Beautiful Weddings

Beautiful Weddings

HUNDREDS OF STYLISH IDEAS FROM THE
WORLD'S MOST STUNNING REAL WEDDINGS

Carole Hamilton

RYLAND
PETERS
& SMALL

LONDON NEW YORK

Senior Designer Amy Trombat
Senior Editor Henrietta Heald
Picture Research Carole Hamilton
Picture Research Coordination Emily Westlake
Production Manager Patricia Harrington
Publishing Director Alison Starling

First published in the USA in 2008
by Ryland Peters & Small, Inc.
519 Broadway
5th Floor
New York, NY 10012
London WC1R 4BW
www.rylandpeters.com

10 9 8 7 6 5 4 3 2 1

ISBN-10: 1-84597-454-9
ISBN-13: 978-1-84597-454-1

Library of Congress Cataloging-in-Publication Data

Hamilton, Carole.
  Beautiful weddings hundreds of stylish ideas from the
world's most stunning real weddings / Carole Hamilton.
      p. cm.
  Includes index.
  ISBN 978-1-84597-454-1
  1. Weddings–Planning. I. Title.
  HQ745.H234 2008
  395.2'2–dc22
                              2007024667

Printed in China

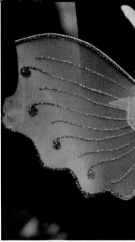

Contents

creating a *Beautiful Wedding*

A beautiful wedding is a visual treat full of surprising little touches that will delight your guests. A beautiful wedding brings together a host of decorative ideas to make a well-coordinated day that perfectly suits the personalities of both the bride and the groom. And creating a beautiful wedding is also a matter of inspired teamwork, when hand-picked suppliers work together to interpret your dreams before turning them into glorious reality.

Every wedding is unique, but what is it that transforms a special occasion into an extra-special one? It's not just a matter of money. A lavish budget will go a long way toward buying the best ingredients, but it is a bride with a dream that makes all the difference.

Before you can begin to plan your own beautiful day, you must define your personal wedding style. Think about the things you love that could play a part. A favorite color palette, a particular flower, a decorative style—any or all of these will help you to form a clearer picture of what you want.

What does your perfect wedding look like in your mind's eye? Is it characterized by an abundance of hearts, flowers, and well-loved traditions or more of a contemporary celebration in a big city hotel? It is important that the venue harmonizes with your chosen theme. Fairies and butterflies are bound to look out of place in a grand ballroom, while traditional linens and crystal are perfectly suited to such a formal setting.

What are your wedding priorities? Make a list, in order of importance, of every element that really matters to you. Include everything from the venue right down to the favors. Once the budget has been set, you may have to compromise on some of the things on your wish list, but at least you will know what is absolutely essential and what you could, at a pinch, do without.

Seasonal harmony

At what time of year are you planning to get married? The season plays a significant part in the style of any wedding. A summer wedding beckons you and your guests to go outdoors to enjoy the sunshine, and a picnic or a party in a tent can be an obvious choice for a summer reception. A winter celebration demands the glow of log fires and candlelight, with guests treated to hearty fare and warming drinks.

Working with, rather than against, the season will also benefit your budget, since seasonal produce is almost always better value than the out-of-season alternatives.

The wedding theme

Do you want your wedding to have a theme? This may sound a little grand, but a theme can be something as simple as using your favorite color as a focal point for flowers and table and room decorations. Or you may want to choose a theme that's personal to the two of you, such as a love of classic films, romantic cities you have visited together, or even a period of history that complements the architecture of your venue. Any beautiful

wedding depends on perfect coordination, and setting a theme will contribute a great deal toward achieving this.

The wedding budget

Once you have put together a clear picture of your dream wedding, the crucial question is: can you afford it? Weddings are expensive, and all but the most lavish celebrations will involve a degree of compromise. To work out your budget, add together your savings, what you think you can save during your engagement, and any family contributions. The total becomes your wedding budget, and all your plans need to work within (or pretty close to) this amount.

A wedding budget can easily get out of hand. The best way to avoid this is through forward planning. Use the formula below to work out roughly what you have to spend on each of the key areas of the wedding.

THE WEDDING BUDGET

40%	Reception, including food and drink
15%	Venue/ceremony
10%	Outfits
10%	Flowers/entertainment/ transportation
7%	Photography/video
3%	Stationery
10%	Honeymoon
5%	Unexpected extras

You can, of course, devote a larger proportion of your budget to one or more particular elements of the wedding, but if you do, you need to make sure you can compensate for it somewhere else. For example, if a designer dress is high on your list of priorities, then you probably won't be able to serve vintage champagne at the reception, and so on.

If you calculate in advance how much money you have to spend, it means that looking at potential venues and discussing what you want with prospective suppliers is likely to be much more straightforward than it would otherwise have been. You can be honest about how much you can afford, and they will find it easier to come up with ideas to suit your means. Beautiful weddings do not have to involve an enormous budget. Imagination and the clever use of what you have are what count.

Your dream team

The venue manager, the caterer, the florist, the photographer, and perhaps a wedding planner are all part of any couple's dream team. These are the wedding experts who will listen to your vision, contribute their own suggestions and ideas, and then take responsibility for making it all come together on time and on budget for the big day.

First and foremost, you are looking for people who share your vision. If prospective suppliers are constantly trying to get you to increase your budget or radically change your ideas, they are probably not the right choice for you. You will be working closely with these people over the months ahead, so you need to get along well with them.

Always insist on seeing samples of a supplier's previous work. In the case of a photographer or a florist, ask if you can see a portfolio. This should consist not simply of carefully chosen one-off shots, but photographs of a whole wedding or a whole set of floral arrangements and bouquets. Consistency is what you're looking for.

There are important questions to consider when visiting potential venues. How flexible does the staff appear? Can they accommodate some of your most unusual ideas? If there is any suggestion that you should change your vision for your big day, it may well prove more satisfactory to look for a different venue.

Be realistic about how much time you can devote to planning your wedding. If you have a hectic lifestyle and perhaps no willing mother to help you, it may be worth considering using the services of a wedding planner. Having somebody to negotiate with suppliers, make sure deadlines are met, and offer neverending support and advice has a lot to be said for it. Wedding planners can be costly, but what they save in time and stress is invaluable for many couples.

Food and drink

When it comes to deciding what food and drink to serve your guests, you need to be certain that any menu tastes as good as it looks. Expect to sample your chosen menu, with accompanying wines, in advance.

Food and drink will absorb the largest slice of your wedding budget, so make sure you are delighted, rather than simply lukewarm, about what is on the proposed menu. If you don't like something, ask to have it changed. Caterers are professionals, and they will not be offended if you want to alter a few ingredients.

Setting the wedding style

Once you have organized the principal elements of the wedding, including choosing the reception venue and appointing your most important suppliers, the fun can really

---

TRIED-AND-TESTED
COLOR THEMES

All white

White and pastel pink

White and hot pink

White and Tiffany blue

White and gold

White and silver

White and black

Red and gold

Fuchsia, lime, and orange

---

begin. Now is the time to decide what your wedding will actually look like.

The best-coordinated weddings always have a theme. Ideally, in considering themes, you should work with the style of the venue as well as with the season.

Visit your chosen venue, preferably in the company of your florist, and make a thorough inspection of the rooms you will be using. What colors are the carpets and draperies? There is nothing you can do to change these, so whatever color scheme you choose needs to harmonize with what's there. For example, if the predominant colors in a room are scarlet and gold, a sugar pink and white theme would look wrong, whereas a white and gold, red and green, or even a hot pink and gold color scheme would all complement the room.

Lighting

Think about the time of the day when the reception will be held so you will know what the light will be like at the venue. Light can make or break the atmosphere at any event, so ideally you need to visit the venue at the same time of year and the same time of day that you will be using it.

If your wedding is being held in winter, the rooms will be dark from mid-afternoon, so ask about the lighting system; all larger venues will have a lighting expert on hand to give you advice and guidance.

Overhead strip lighting can look very harsh and is better suited to a conference than a wedding. Can lights be dimmed? Are there wall lights available that emit a softer light? Are you allowed to use candlelight at the venue? Candles undoubtedly offer the most romantic light, but be warned: because of safety considerations, many historical buildings won't allow naked flames.

If you are marrying in summer, you will, with any luck, have sunshine streaming in through the windows, but are there sheer curtains to shield guests from direct sunlight? Can larger windows and doors be opened? Does the venue have air conditioning?

Flowers and decorations

When it comes to decorating the reception room, less is usually more. Don't feel that you have to cover every surface with flowers; often a few well-placed arrangements are more effective than lots of smaller, and often more expensive, centerpieces.

Stand in the doorway of the dining room and imagine what it would look like when filled with tables. Which areas catch your eye? Is there a focal point in the room such as a fireplace that demands decoration? Where is the best place to set up the cake table so that guests can admire it without it being knocked over? Is there anything unsightly and, if so, how can you cover it up?

Work with the venue manager on the room layout. Since he or she is likely to have seen the room dressed in many different ways, the manager should be a good source of inspiration. For a large wedding, make sure there is enough space between the tables and between the chairs at each table for guests to feel comfortable. For a smaller wedding, you need to make good use of the room to prevent it from looking empty, as though half your guests haven't turned up! Separating the room into different sections with colorful screens is one solution. Another is hanging up nets of fairy lights to create a separate dance-floor area.

Using round tables for a wedding feast is traditional, but if it's feasible, consider having one or two very long tables with just one small rectangular table as the top table. There is nothing quite as dramatic as seeing a single table laid for, say, fifty guests lined with candelabra and decorated with colorful touches such as napkins, favors, and flowers. Instant impact for little effort!

The great outdoors

Finally, don't forget about outside space. This won't be so relevant if yours is a winter wedding, but at other times of the year a patio area or garden offers a lot of scope for entertaining your guests. In summer put up white market umbrellas to provide welcome shade or erect a few colorful Raj-style tents complete with piles of comfortable cushions to create a picnic theme.

Visit your local garden center for inspiration. Buying decorative items often works out cheaper than renting them, and you can always sell what you don't want to keep after the wedding. Encourage guests to come outside on balmy summer evenings by stringing fairy lights in the trees, hanging ornamental lanterns from low branches, and lining walkways with flaming torches. Chinese paper lanterns are colorful and cheap to buy and look very effective dancing in a summer breeze.

Creating a wow factor

However simple your wedding style, try to incorporate an element that will make the guests say "Wow!" when they arrive. Favorite ideas include a bubbling chocolate fountain, an ice sculpture, a tower of individual cupcakes, or a room lit solely by candlelight or filled with an abundance of scented white flowers. But remember that your wedding will be memorable if, above all, it is full of personal touches and genuinely reflects the lifestyle and personalities of the bride and groom. Have fun!

The highlights of every traditional wedding are the classic details: crystal, linen, and fine china in abundance, creating a feeling of elegance and style. Traditional weddings effortlessly blend well-loved customs with modern touches to reflect the personalities of the bride and groom.

Traditional

elegant wedding *Under the Stars*

The spectacular Villa Vizcaya is the perfect setting for a wedding that exudes elegance and glamour. It was the first choice of venue for the black-tie nuptials between watch designer Michele Barouh and lawyer Jeffrey Erez.

Inspired by the Italian Renaissance, the Baroque architecture of Villa Vizcaya leads you to believe that the building is overlooking the Italian lakes, whereas it is actually on Biscayne Bay in Miami, Florida. For a wedding at such an impressive venue, the colors should reflect the decor of the building. Michele chose an orange and blue theme to harmonize with the villa's dramatic shades of coral, turquoise, beige, and gold. She came up with most of the creative ideas herself, along with her mother and best friend, but she had one of Florida's leading event organizers on hand to give advice.

The couple wanted the big day to look elegant, classic, and timeless, so the dress code for the 200 guests at the early evening ceremony was black tie, giving everyone a chance to dress up in their finery. The bride wore a stunning Vera Wang couture dress made from yards of ivory ribbon. She maintains that she tried on every wedding dress in New York before deciding on the very first one she had seen! The ceremony was held in the gardens of the villa, with the couple exchanging their vows beneath a breathtaking archway of white flowers. The aisle was a white carpet lined with lanterns, and guests sat on golden chairs with white cushions. Michele only had one attendant, her male best friend, Josh, who wore a tuxedo.

An enormous white tent with a dramatic ceiling was the setting for the reception. There were flowers everywhere—literally thousands of individual blooms arranged in a variety of silver vases lining the reception tables. Guests were seated at one long table that ran the

ABOVE Villa Vizcaya is a Renaissance-style museum with wrap-around terraces, making it ideal for an evening reception. OPPOSITE, ABOVE The outdoor ceremony was held at sunset with the bride and groom walking up a white-carpeted aisle lit by dozens of lamps. OPPOSITE, BELOW LEFT Guests were asked to write messages of good luck onto cards and stick them onto silver twigs to make a "memory tree" on the terrace. OPPOSITE, BELOW RIGHT The couple's initials were a main theme of the day. They were used on the stationery, to decorate the cake, and in a spotlight on the dance floor.

length of the room, with smaller rectangular tables on each side to accommodate the sheer number of people. The tables were dressed in periwinkle-blue linen with silver flatware and silver-edged crystal sparkling in the candlelight. Running the length of each table were vibrant orange arrangements of tulips, freesias, roses, and miniature calla lilies. Enormous stone urns, sprayed silver and packed with a abundance of lilac hydrangeas, stood on top of silver stone columns lining the tent. Each place setting featured a menu, a linen napkin, a favor box of specially selected chocolates, and, for female guests, a camellia. The menu had a Mediterranean influence to reflect the style of the venue; guests dined on sea bass and fillets accompanied by fine wines and vintage champagne.

One nice touch, which meant a lot to the couple, was the "best wishes tree." Guests were asked to write cards offering congratulations and advice for the future to the newlyweds;

LEFT The wedding reception was held in a spectacular tent with a draped ceiling. The main guest table ran the length of the space and seated more than 100 people; smaller rectangular tables lined each side. Each table had a periwinkle-blue tablecloth and was decorated with vibrant orange arrangements using roses, freesias, orchids, and calla lilies in silver vases that twinkled in the candlelight. Silver-sprayed stone urns of lilac hydrangeas were dotted throughout the tent, topping silver-sprayed stone columns. **BELOW** Each place setting included a menu incorporating the couple's entwined initials and a box of their favorite chocolates. The female guests each had a camellia flower.

Dress to Impress A black-tie wedding is a stylish option, especially if the wedding is held late in the day or in winter when it gets dark early. Guests revel in the chance to dress up, and the formality always looks great in the wedding photographs. State your chosen dress code on the invitations. Black tie means a tuxedo for the men and evening dress for the women. Formal means morning dress or dark suits for the men and cocktail wear and hats for the women. If you don't specify a dress code, guests can suit themselves, while still keeping to wedding attire.

ABOVE Just one of the many wow! factors at this wedding were the silver-sprayed urns on silver columns that lined the tent, each brimming with lilac hydrangeas.
ABOVE RIGHT The four-tier wedding cake was decorated with the couple's initials and topped with a miniature posy of sugar stephanotis flowers. The cake was surrounded by lilac hydrangeas.

these were then pushed onto silver twigs in one of the hydrangea urns on the terrace. By the end of the evening, the twigs were covered in a mass of cards that have since been put into a wedding album. The couple's entwined initials were a recurring theme of the day; they were used on all the stationery and to decorate the wedding cake. During the evening, their initials were spotlit on the dance floor and the outside terrace as guests danced under the stars.

There are various ways to get your guests to record good wishes for the future. A simple guest book and pen can be left at the entrance to the reception, or you can put a Polaroid camera on a "memory table," where each guest or couple takes their picture, sticks it into a book, and writes a message next to the picture. Alternatively, ask your videographer's assistant to roam the room getting messages on camera to make a DVD you can keep. For many couples, their guests' good wishes compiled at the wedding become a treasured possession.

As guests left Michele and Jeffrey's wedding, everyone was given a limited-edition watch from Michele's latest collection, either in orange or blue to suit the color scheme, each one engraved with the couple's names and wedding date on the back.

castle wedding *A Love of Lilac*

Inspiration for a theme can be as simple as a color, a flower, or, as in the case of this bride, shoes! Tiny lilac heels adorned everything from the stationery to the wedding cake at this sumptuous celebration at a castle in the English countryside.

When Sonita Madhar and Jonathan Gale decided to get married at Highclere Castle, they could have easily let the wonderful Victorian architecture of the building speak for itself. But Sonita, whose family roots are in India, was determined to stamp her personality on the day and—inspired by the work of fashion illustrator Nicky Belton—came up with the shoe theme. The lilac shoes along with a beautiful pale pink rose determined the color scheme for all the many style details and decorations. For anyone seeking a theme on which to base a wedding, the best way to find inspiration is to think about the things you love.

Sonita and Jonathan wanted to create a day of love and laughter for their family and friends that reflected the coming together of the Indian and British cultures. This delighted their guests, many of whom had traveled from distant parts of the world to join their celebrations. Guests were welcomed at the door by two heart-shaped wreaths tied with lilac ribbon and adorned with lilac shoes. One lilac-potted rosemary plant stood on either side of the door, each tied with fabric taken from the same bolt of cloth that made Sonita's 1940s-inspired wedding dress.

The wedding ceremony was held in the castle great hall, and the room was filled with pots of pale pink Candy Bianca roses and lilac hydrangeas. Fresh pink rose petals were scattered the length of the imposing staircase, and garlands of roses and gardenia hung from the balustrades delicately scenting the air. Sonita's bouquet was made of Candy Bianca and Metallina roses with rhinestone studs that twinkled in the light. Her three bridesmaids carried lilac bags covered

Scent from Heaven Fragrance plays an important part at a wedding, helping to create lasting memories for all the guests. Ask your florist to include some highly scented blooms in the arrangements at the ceremony and the reception, as well as in the bride's bouquet and the groom's boutonniere. Traditional favorites include gardenia, stephanotis, lily of the valley, calla lilies, roses, and hyacinths. Strongly scented herbs such as the rosemary bushes Sonita used at the entrance also add to an evocative atmosphere. The couple left the ceremony under a shower of scented rose-petal confetti, walking under an archway decorated with pink blossom and hydrangeas.

LEFT Highclere Castle in Berkshire, England, was the spectacular wedding venue. It stands on the site of an earlier house dating back to medieval times, when it was home to the Bishops of Winchester. It is now the home of the Earl of Carnarvon. ABOVE Sonita's three bridesmaids wore lilac dresses and carried lilac bucket-style handbags filled with pink roses. ABOVE RIGHT Guests entered the castle through a door flanked by potted rosemary trees and decorated with foliage hearts on lilac ribbons.

with sequins and filled with the same pink roses. At the reception, all the tables featured an arrangement of pink and beige roses, lilac hydrangeas, and calla lilies displayed in a pale pink wax bowl, specially chosen to match the pink of the bride's dress.

Guests were treated to a menu of Indian delights prepared by one of London's premier Indian caterers, including chicken kabobs in peppercorn and garlic marinade, tiger prawns in yogurt, and lamb in ginger and coriander. Dessert was a mango kulfi, a type of Indian ice cream, and coffee was served with slices from the spectacular white chocolate cake.

Sonita and Jonathan, who had taken secret dancing lessons before the wedding, put on a professional performance for their first dance, to Dusty Springfield's "The Look of Love." The evening ended as they made a dramatic exit, driving away from the castle in a vintage Rolls–Royce against a backdrop of spectacular fireworks exploding across the night sky.

And finally, many of Sonita's friends were so impressed by how well the wedding had been organized that they asked her to help with their weddings. She has since set up a thriving wedding planning business of her own!

RIGHT The centerpieces for the reception tables were pale pink wax bowls filled with pink and beige roses, lilies, and lilac hydrangeas. **OPPOSITE, ABOVE** Nicky Belton, a fashion illustrator, provided the inspiration for the wedding's shoes theme. Examples of her work were laid alongside the placecards at the entrance to the reception venue. **OPPOSITE, BELOW LEFT** The white chocolate cake was covered with pink chocolate roses, lilac chocolate leaves and, of course, lilac chocolate shoes. The cake table was covered with fresh petals. **OPPOSITE, BELOW RIGHT** Each bridesmaid carried a sequin-covered handbag filled with Candy Bianca roses and decorated with tiny shoes.

city wedding *Classic Glamour*

San Francisco, one of the world's most romantic cities, is brimming with amazing venues. Fashion stylist and television presenter Katie Rice loved showing off its delights to guests from around the U.S. before her wedding there to Bradley Jones.

The rehearsal cocktail party was held in the Swig Penthouse at the famous Fairmont Hotel with its panoramic views over the city, and the marriage ceremony was conducted at St. Dominic's Catholic Church. The evening reception venue was the elegant Old Federal Reserve building. With its huge rooms and high ceilings, it was the perfect location for the black-tie dinner and dance that the couple wanted.

Silhouettes of the couple's heads were hand-embossed on all the stationery, from the invitations to the menu cards. Each invitation was handwritten and included a hand-drawn map of the wedding locations. The color scheme for the day was ecru, blush pink, and black. Katie introduced intimate touches by wearing her mother's restyled wedding dress at the rehearsal party along with her paternal grandmother's jewelry. On her wedding day she wore her maternal grandmother's diamond and ruby watch and cameo necklace.

Something old, something new, something borrowed, something blue . . . . Many brides want to uphold this tradition on their wedding day. The easiest way to do so is to incorporate mementoes from family, past and present. Katie used jewelry and her mother's wedding dress, but other possibilities include a family Bible or prayer book, a family veil—or perhaps wrapping your bouquet in a piece of vintage wedding dress fabric. For something new and blue, ask your dress designer to sew a tiny blue ribbon into the hem of your wedding gown.

ABOVE Handmade stationery featuring embossed silhouettes of the couple added a personal touch to the reception tables. **OPPOSITE, ABOVE LEFT** Katie, wearing a strapless Palazzo dress, is surrounded by flower girls in pink Laura Ashley dresses. **OPPOSITE, ABOVE RIGHT** The flower girls' accessories were black sashes and black bows. **OPPOSITE, BELOW LEFT** Brad wore black tie and a boutonniere of stephanotis flowers. **OPPOSITE, BELOW RIGHT** The bride carried a peony bouquet and wore her grandmother's watch as an example of "something old."

The evening began with a wine and champagne reception in an intimate, curtained-off section of the Old Federal Reserve's lobby. Dinner was announced by the bride's 10-year-old nephew playing the tune of the German song "Morsch" on a glockenspiel. The round tables were dressed with classic linens, crystal glasses, and silverware. Table numbers and the individual menus at each place setting both bore the couple's silhouette design. The wine bottles all had customized labels, again using the silhouettes and the wedding date.

The menu consisted of a salad with champagne vinaigrette followed by a trio of grilled sirloin, lavender salmon, and eggplant tart. After dinner came the wedding cake, designed to match Katie's dress and flowers, and the party was rounded off with a vodka bar serving drinks named after different sights in San Francisco.

LEFT Guests were greeted at their tables with a handwritten menu bearing silhouettes of the bride and groom. **BELOW LEFT** Pink and white peonies in classic silver vases made up the centerpieces. The reception was full of such stylish touches, which gave the event a look of elegance and glamour without excessive formality. **OPPOSITE, ABOVE LEFT AND RIGHT** The three-tiered cake was designed to look like the bride's dress, emulating the pleating and decorated with lots of sugar stephanotis flowers. It was topped with a fresh peony. **OPPOSITE, BELOW LEFT** Peonies, in shades of cream and pink, were the main flowers used throughout the day for the bride's bouquet and the table arrangements. **OPPOSITE, BELOW RIGHT** The guests selected their table numbers from cards arranged in a flower shape inside three stone urns. Each urn contained different letters of the alphabet so guests could easily find their names.

A Sense of Style

A historic building can be a good choice of venue for a big wedding with a large number of guests, but don't forget to make sure it is suitable for your dream day. A period property is often governed by rules about what, if anything, you can move around, and you will probably be allowed only limited access to the building. Naked flames may be forbidden, in which case a romantic candlelit reception would be a non-starter. But, on the plus side, this style of venue makes a dramatic impact. The rooms are likely to have grand and elegant proportions with wonderful high ceilings and a sense of history—all of which are all bound to impress your guests.

valley wedding *Summer Sunshine*

"Quel beau lieu!," French for "How beautiful!," were the first words uttered by Fernande de Latour in 1900, when she saw the property her husband, Georges, planned to buy in the Napa Valley—and the name stuck. The garden at Beaulieu is now one of northern California's most popular wedding venues.

Stephanie Kelmar and Raphael Reich live in San Francisco and have always loved exploring the glorious Napa Valley wine country at weekends, so a wine estate was a natural choice for their summer nuptials. The wedding was an Orthodox Jewish ceremony held beside a lake with their guests seated around them, shaded from the strong midday sun by colorful parasols. Their florist, Julie Stevens, was closely involved in creating the overall style of the wedding; she chose a color palette of deep reds, burgundy, and spicy orange to complement the rich colors and textures of the wine country.

The *chuppah* poles were made from birch and decorated with masses of deep red climbing roses. The bride's hand-tied bouquet was a mixture of deep red Classy roses, spicy orange roses, and flame-colored miniature calla lilies. It was surrounded with angel vine and tied with a pearl-encrusted ribbon.

The table centerpieces used square glass vases wrapped with sheer gold organza fabric to complement the table linen. Most containers for table centerpieces are made from clear glass, which means the flower stems are always on show. To disguise this and add another splash of color, wrap each container in a fabric to match your theme or, alternatively, fill each container with colored pebbles or marbles before arranging the flowers.

ABOVE The couple exchanged vows in a traditional Jewish ceremony at Beaulieu Gardens in California's Napa Valley. **OPPOSITE, ABOVE LEFT AND RIGHT** The guests' handwritten name cards were put into four ribbon-trimmed boxes filled with orange flower petals and displayed on a table under a vine-covered walkway. **OPPOSITE, BELOW LEFT** The couple's *ketubah* (Jewish marriage certificate) is written in Hebrew script and decorated with a floral design. **OPPOSITE, BELOW RIGHT** The flower girls wore dresses in cream and green and carried fresh rose petals in tiny baskets. The bridesmaids wore black dresses and carried posies of orange roses.

OPPOSITE Stephanie and Raphael made their vows beneath a traditional *chuppah* decorated with a mass of interwoven climbing roses. **ABOVE** Each centerpiece consisted of Vanda orchids, Black Bacarra roses, spicy orange roses, and hypericum berries surrounded by scented geranium leaves and angel vine, all contained in an organza-covered vase. **ABOVE RIGHT** The three-tiered cake was studded with sugar pearls and decorated with fresh roses to match the table decorations. **ABOVE, FAR RIGHT** The bride's bouquet was a mixture of deep red Classy roses, spicy orange roses, and miniature calla lilies. It was surrounded by angel vine and tied with pearl-encrusted ribbon.

Stephanie and Raphael's wedding was characterized by a mood of relaxed simplicity. The reception was held in a courtyard, shaded by the branches of a dozen trees. The tables were dressed with cream and beige linens with tangerine-trimmed napkins and peach-colored glasses to match the orange tones of the floral centerpieces. Guests enjoyed cocktails under the trees to a musical accompaniment from a string quartet.

The wedding feast consisted of a delightful summer menu of salad with spiced pecans, pears, and blue cheese followed by a choice of either fillet of beef, grilled chicken breast, or a Tuscan vegetable terrine. Dessert was blackberry cabernet sorbet with fresh berries served in a martini glass with summer flower petals and a ring of butter cookies. A selection of red, white, and sparkling wine from the Beaulieu estate accompanied the meal.

Flowers were also used to decorate the three-tiered wedding cake, a wickedly delicious concoction of vanilla-bean pound cake filled with crushed apricot preserves and vanilla butter, cream and yellow cake with white chocolate mousse and raspberries.

The remainder of the wedding day was spent relaxing in the afternoon sunshine with family and friends, and enjoying traditional *hora* dancing until sunset.

LEFT An outside reception is all about creating a welcoming space where your guests will enjoy dining. On this occasion, the reception was held in a courtyard under the cooling shade of a dozen trees. The framework of the gazebo was entwined with fairy lights to create a magical atmosphere after dark. The round tables were dressed in a relaxed, country style with beige and cream swirled linens and low centerpieces of roses and lilies. **BELOW** Place settings included napkins with a tangerine trim and colored wine glasses that tied in perfectly with the color theme.

fall wedding *Mellow Fruitfulness*

A seasonal theme is traditionally one of the most successful ways to coordinate a wedding, bringing together the color palettes of nature with fresh local flowers and seasonal produce.

The rich and sumptuous shades of the fall proved an irresistible attraction for Kristin Feyen and Daniel Glunt when they began to think about a theme for their dream wedding in a San Francisco mansion.

Giving your wedding a theme is always an excellent idea if you want to convey an impression of harmony and coordination. Using a color theme is an obvious choice, and opting for a seasonal color scheme is even better, whether it is blossom pink and fresh green in spring, dazzling white and sky blue for summer or, as in this case, the glorious rich russets and oranges of the fall.

Kristin and Dan's shared passion for travel was used to personalize certain elements of their wedding, but they both also love the colors of the fall, which was one reason why they chose to have a September wedding. All the flowers and table details were from a bright palette: champagne, warm brown, rich red, rose red, and sunburst orange.

After a religious ceremony at the Episcopal Church of St. Mary the Virgin, guests were invited to board traditional San Francisco cable cars for the journey up the steep hills of Pacific Heights to the spectacular James Leary Flood Mansion, the venue chosen for the reception. The mansion, built in the 1920s, is a wonderful example of American domestic architecture, combining Rococo, Georgian, and Renaissance design styles with spectacular views from its lofty position above San Francisco Bay.

ABOVE Guests travelled to the reception in traditional San Francisco cable cars. **OPPOSITE, LEFT** The bridesmaids wore strapless black dresses and carried posies of fall flowers. **OPPOSITE, ABOVE RIGHT** The bride's bouquet was secured by a strip of rich bronze fabric studded with pearls. **OPPOSITE, BELOW LEFT** The bride and groom share a quiet moment before boarding the cable car for the reception.

While the bride and groom were spirited away for a photography session, each of their guests was offered a Mojito cocktail, the groom's favorite tipple and an acknowledgment of his Cuban heritage. For the reception, the guests were seated on gold chairs at circular tables covered with rust- and rose-colored linens.

Each of the tables at the reception had a low centerpiece arrangement of miniature roses, hydrangeas, and calla lilies; all were various shades of orange and russet and chosen to coordinate with the bride's bouquet of roses and calla lilies and the bridesmaids' autumnal posies. In keeping with the mansion theme, all the placecard holders were tiny antique chairs that doubled as favors for guests to take home as a memento.

ABOVE The centerpieces for the reception tables combined hydrangeas, calla lilies, and miniature roses with green and rich brown foliage. **ABOVE CENTER** The four-tier cake was a concoction of chocolate, mint, and raspberry covered in white fondant icing. **ABOVE FAR RIGHT** Posies of hydrangeas tied with russet ribbons were suspended from the branches of trees to form an arch for the couple's arrival at the reception. **LEFT** Each of the tables was dressed in shades of orange and russet and named for a city that the couple had visited during their extensive travels. The view from the windows across the bay to Alcatraz was spectacular.

Nothing makes Kristin and Daniel happier than jetting off around the world with their packs on their backs, so every table was named after one of their favorite destinations. Each table also had a collage of photographs telling a visual story of a memorable trip. Friends from out of town who had been visited by Kristin and Dan in their home city generally found themselves sitting at tables named after that city.

Guests feasted on a delicious menu of tomato salad, Alaskan halibut, and blackened fillet mignon with tropical mango salsa. For dessert, waiters served individual miniature chocolate soufflés, and the chef, Patrick David, delighted guests with plates of his famous homemade truffles. The wedding cake was tiered layers of white chocolate and raspberry alternating with layers of chocolate mint covered in white fondant icing.

The couple's first dance was to Van Morrison's "Into the Mystic." Just before they left the reception, instead of the traditional toss of the bouquet by the bride, Kristin decided to give her bouquet to the couple who had been married the longest. She turned the selection process into a game. All the married couples were asked to stand up and then to sit down if they had been married for less than one year, five years, ten years, and so on. High-school sweethearts who had been married for 36 years were the eventual winners.

weekend wedding *Beach Paradise*

For a perfect example of a thoroughly modern celebration in beautiful surroundings, this wedding weekend in St. Tropez is hard to beat. Susanne Thomas and Darren Shipard shared a sublime few days of sun, sea, sport, and feasting with family and friends; their wedding was the icing on the cake.

For a couple based in London, both lovers of sunshine and sailing, the choice of wedding location was easy. The South of France had long been a favorite sailing destination, and they had met at a regatta in St. Tropez two years earlier. The area had all the elements the couple could hope for, including the fabulous Villa Belrose, the venue for the wedding party.

The weekend started on a Thursday evening with drinks on the Villa Belrose terrace. All the guests had welcome bags in their rooms including a personalized itinerary based on the activities they had chosen (such as wine tasting, sailing, beach-bar party, night clubbing), maps and information on the area, and a CD of Susanne and Darren's favorite music.

Friday was spent sailing or visiting a local vineyard, and guests then met up at a local beach bar for late afternoon drinks, volleyball, and swimming. A special champagne cocktail, dedicated to the couple and called the King Cole Llama Punch, was served before a dinner of fresh local seafood. Afterward the two best men presented a slide show of Darren's life and produced a collage of photographs of the couple, which all the guests were asked to sign as a memento. The evening concluded at the Caves du Roy nightclub, a celebrity haunt.

The theme for the wedding day itself was an abundance of bright color; the couple chose a combination of pink and yellow roses and pink lighting to enhance the party atmosphere. Style details included topiary trees and large arrangements of white roses for

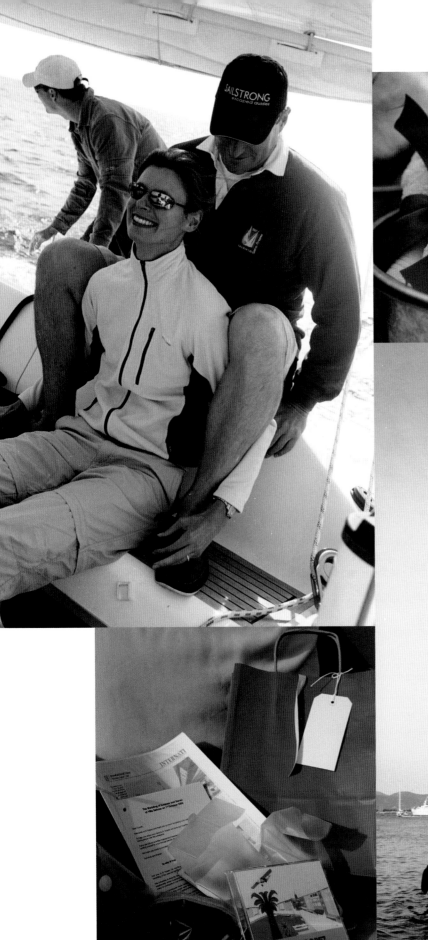

ABOVE The evening before the wedding was given over to beach volleyball and swimming, followed by a delicious seafood dinner. **OPPOSITE, ABOVE LEFT** The couple enjoyed a pre-wedding sailing trip in the St. Tropez sunshine. **LEFT AND OPPOSITE, BELOW RIGHT** The sailing theme was a feature of the occasion, with miniature sails acting as name tags for each guest. **OPPOSITE, ABOVE RIGHT** Towels wrapped in ribbons were placed in buckets on the walkways to freshen sandy feet. **OPPOSITE, BELOW LEFT** A personalized weekend bag was given to each guest containing a CD, itinerary, local information, and candy.

ABOVE The Mediterranean splendor of the Villa Belrose was the backdrop for the wedding celebrations. **OPPOSITE, ABOVE** Guests were entertained during pre-dinner drinks by a local jazz quartet. After dinner, a ten-piece band took over and provided dance music into the night. **OPPOSITE, BELOW RIGHT** The entrance to the ceremony venue was adorned by voile-covered topiary trees. **OPPOSITE, BELOW LEFT** Susanne and Darren enjoy a quiet moment on a beachside daybed.

the ceremony; yellow and white rose petals were scattered up the aisle. The bride arrived to "You and Me" from the movie *Romeo and Juliet*, and the couple left to the strains of Barry White's "My First, My Last, My Everything."

At the reception the seating cards were made to look like sails, stuck on wooden poles and arranged in buckets of sand with the guests' names on one side and their table numbers on the other. All the tables were named after towns in the area, such as St. Tropez, Cannes, and Nice. Menu covers featured an old poster image of St. Tropez that was the same image used on the wedding invitations and the ceremony order of service.

Guests dined on langoustines with grated summer truffles, mignon of beef with seasonal vegetables, a selection of cheeses, and a dessert of red fruit and almond milk, flavored with grapefruit and served with mango sorbet. The cake was a trio of traditional sachertortes.

St. Tropez

LEFT The feathered showgirls from the Paris Lido were a surprise, but welcome, addition to the evening's entertainments. **BELOW LEFT** Susanne and Darren stood on a carpet of rose petals to have their marriage blessed in front of family and friends. **OPPOSITE, ABOVE LEFT AND RIGHT** The reception tables were dressed in white; at their center were candelabra topped with dramatic balls of yellow and pink roses and trailing ivy. **OPPOSITE, BELOW LEFT** Each table was named after a different French town in the area. **OPPOSITE, BELOW RIGHT** The cake—a trio of sachertortes—was specially bought and delivered from the originators of the delicacy, the Hotel Sacher in Vienna.

showgirl surprise

A highlight of the evening was the arrival of a troupe of Lido showgirls from Paris, who performed a routine from *Chicago*—the groom had been living in Chicago, and many of the guests were from the city. The girls finished the dance with the traditional Paris Lido topless act!

seaside wedding *Hilltop Heaven*

This celebration on a hill overlooking Italy's dramatic Amalfi coast is the ultimate destination wedding, marking the union between a Japanese bride and a Chinese–American groom. Reiko Arakawa and Richard Liaw chose Hotel Caruso in Ravello as the perfect place for their wedding.

The invitations were sourced in Amalfi and then dressed with traditional Japanese unryu tissue and gold metallic midare paper. A wax seal of the Chinese double happiness symbol (a traditional Chinese wedding sign) completed the ensemble. The color theme for the day was red, the traditional color for Asian weddings, and many of the guests carried red parasols to shade themselves from the fierce Mediterranean sun.

The day began when a private coach picked up the guests from their hotels and villas on the coast and dropped them off near Ravello's town square. They were met by two mandolin players, who escorted them through the streets to the venue. As they walked along, townspeople clapped and cheered, while, coincidentally, fireworks exploded in the distance.

The marriage ceremony took place outdoors under a sheer white *tentilino*, or portable awning, supported on green bamboo poles and adorned with strings of flowers. Each corner pole was held by a close friend of the bride and groom, representing pillars of love, support, and friendship. The groom's sister wrote a special poem entitled "Wedding Wishes" and read it as part of the ceremony. Afterward, her children, the groom's niece and nephew, surprised the guests by giving their own rendition of the song "Somewhere Over the Rainbow."

Described by the couple as "Asian alfresco," the reception was held in the hotel gardens. Ribbonlike menus decorated each plate, adorned with red Chinese coin pouches holding a

ABOVE The wedding party strolled through Ravello to the venue serenaded by two mandolin players, as local people clapped and cheered. **OPPOSITE, ABOVE LEFT** The couple got married under a *tentilino* whose supporting bamboo poles were covered with garlands of local flowers. **OPPOSITE, BELOW LEFT** The bride's bouquet contained white roses and foliage dotted with miniature white and yellow orchids. **OPPOSITE, ABOVE RIGHT** The flower girl scattered fresh petals up the aisle. Her elder brother shielded her from the sun with a red parasol. **OPPOSITE, BELOW RIGHT** All the guests sat at one long table laid with a green (for good luck) runner and decorated with vases of yellow and white orchids.

placecard with each guest's name handwritten in gold. All the guests dined at one long outdoor table decorated with a green Chinese silk runner, pale yellow and white orchids in tall thin vases, and small candles, votives, and orchids in water. There was a single round table that symbolized unity and harmony, referring to a Chinese wedding tradition.

Guest favors were red Chinese fans printed with the double happiness sign and fans with the Chinese character *Fu* (for good luck). Everyone was also given bottles of Tuscan olive oil strung with a small pouch of traditional Italian bomboniere, consisting of sugared almonds bought locally in Ravello, and a small thank-you card from the bride and groom printed with a haiku poem written by the famous Edo-period haiku master, Basho Matsuo.

Freestanding torches were placed around the table and throughout the grounds to provide light and create a warm atmosphere as the sun set during dinner. The traditional Italian lemon cake was served with champagne beside the swimming pool as guests danced under the stars to a local jazz band.

Venue with a View ... Destination weddings are a popular option for many couples wanting to celebrate their marriage in a suitably fabulous setting away from home. Beach weddings in the Caribbean and Indian Ocean have been the traditional choice, but the latest trend is to hold the celebrations in a historic European location. Italy is the number one destination for romantics and, with venues like this one in Ravello on the Amalfi coast, it is easy to understand why. If you are thinking of planning your own destination wedding, you may find the services of a wedding organizer invaluable. Planning any event long-distance is time-consuming, and a professional with local knowledge will definitely be able to save you time, and often money, as well as helping with the legalities.

For the ultimate fairytale occasion, the romantic wedding has to be fit for a princess bride. Captivated by a venue brimming with decorative touches such as hearts, angels, and flowers, guests will be left in no doubt that this is a day full of love and good wishes.

Romantic

vintage wedding *Tea and Roses*

Romance is not necessarily all about hearts and pink flowers, as Alex Teal showed in her wonderfully individual summer wedding to Tim Holt in Yorkshire, nothern England. She decorated the reception venue in vintage ivory, so that guests would feel as if they were walking into a dreamy and whimsical scene.

Alex's love of old-fashioned glamour made it easy for her to choose a theme for her big day, but it also involved an enormous amount of work. Every detail had to be individually sourced, which meant Alex and her business partner, Amanda Koster, scouring antique markets in London for weeks before the wedding, buying up anything vintage, romantic, eclectic, and fun that could work on the reception tables. The duo had recently set up an event-styling company, and the wedding was the perfect opportunity to show off what they could do. The result was that each table had its own unique theme based on, for example, a one-of-a-kind birdcage, vintage teacups, a tailor's dummy, a 1920s mirror, old Chanel perfume bottles, vintage shoes, jewelry.

Alex and Amanda even sourced the flowers themselves, getting up at 4 A.M. a couple of days before the wedding to search New Covent Garden's famous flower market for a selection of orchids, hydrangeas, roses, and peonies. And the work involved in such a highly decorative project also meant that friends and members of the couple's families were needed to help with the preparations. Even on the morning of the wedding, one of the bridesmaids was spray-painting the chandeliers, and various friends were frantically polishing the silverware and writing name tags before getting dressed for the ceremony!

ABOVE AND OPPOSITE, BELOW RIGHT
The flowergirls were dressed to look
like fairies, complete with wings on their
dresses and daisy circlets on their heads.
OPPOSITE, ABOVE RIGHT With a tie,
waistcoat, and handkerchief in pale pink,
the groom chose a pink rose boutonniere
to match his bride's bouquet. **OPPOSITE,
ABOVE LEFT** The bridesmaids wore feather
butterflies in their hair to complement
their antique eyelet dresses. **OPPOSITE,
BELOW LEFT** The chocolate wedding cake
was iced in cream-colored frosting and
decorated with rows of fresh cream roses.

The reception was held in a tent, so the couple could make the day as personal as possible. Alex and Tim wanted to have a wedding celebration that was totally unique, and the tent gave them the maximum opportunity to make every touch their own.

The ethereal theme that Alex had chosen was reflected in everything from the outfits to the wedding cake. For example, the color of the tent was a soft off-white rather than classic white and, with the addition of cream carpets and whitewashed bamboo dining chairs, the scene was set for a magical celebration. The room sparkled with strings of fairy lights, and candles and votives were used everywhere to create a warm glow as night fell. But it was the tables that really showed off the bride's creative flair.

Each table was given a personal theme that told a different story. For example, "Dressing for Dinner" was a nod to Alex's love of fashion, and the table was decorated with an antique tailor's dummy, feathers, pearls, perfume bottles, and antique-looking traditional roses. Another table had a seashore theme, with white Phalaenopsis orchids and lumps of coral interspersed with white votive holders and soft gray pebbles. All of these decorative items were displayed on pieces of mirror for maximum effect.

ABOVE The four bridesmaids wore vintage slip-dresses with butterflies in their hair. The flowergirls wore fairy wings from a ballet shop and fresh daisy chains as headdresses. ABOVE RIGHT The bridal bouquet consisted of the palest pink roses tightly bunched into a simple hand-held posy. LEFT Inspired by the dress worn by Isadora Duncan in *Swan Lake* in the 1920s, Alex's wedding dress had a tight bodice and a romantic full skirt of strips of tulle, billowing ribbons, and feathers.

The fairytale theme was an essential element of the day. The bride chose a strapless dress with a full, feathery skirt that floated in the breeze; it was inspired by the dress worn by the ballerina Isadora Duncan in *Swan Lake* in the 1920s. She carried a bouquet of pale pink old-fashioned roses. Tim wore a classic morning suit accessorized with a soft pink waistcoat and tie, the rose in his buttonhole matching the roses in Alex's bouquet.

The couple were married in the local church before entertaining their guests at a champagne reception in the flower-filled garden of the bride's parents' home. The bride's mother, who has her own restaurant, happily took charge of the wedding menu: canapés served on vintage mirrors followed by a three-course meal of mozzarella and baby tomato, fillet steak or poached salmon, and an assiette of five desserts.

After the meal came no fewer than seven speeches, and the couple took to the floor to what must be one of the latest first-dance performances ever; they danced to Sting's "Fields of Gold" at 3.30 A.M.—and most of their friends were still there to cheer them on!

Vintage Romance If you want to create a day full of personal touches, a "blank canvas" venue such as a tent or empty hall is often the best choice. You don't have to compete with the decorative style of a traditional room and can add color as and where you want it. Be warned: it does mean you have to bring everything into the venue—and that sometimes includes lighting and a dance floor—and clear it all away again afterward. But, if you can take on the work, the results are nearly always spectacular and well worth the extra effort.

LEFT The seashore theme chosen for this table was defined by a centerpiece of white roses and orchids, a lump of coral, and a scattering of pebbles. **ABOVE** A passion for antiques is reflected in this table setting of vintage beads, hand-held mirrors, and a classic vase filled with long-stemmed roses. **ABOVE RIGHT** Alex's love of fashion meant she couldn't resist including a table covered with vintage Chanel perfume bottles, strings of pearls, and thrift-store teacups, each one filled with soft pink and white roses. **RIGHT** This table had as its centerpiece a white birdcage containing an arrangement of white roses as well as long fronds of ivy. The birdcage was topped with a pair of model white doves.

fantasy wedding *Flight of Fancy*

The inspiration for this London wedding was *Swan Lake* by Tchaikovsky, the bride's favorite composer. It was a lovely theme for a day filled with romance, and Natalia Kudimova and Viorel Campeanu certainly gave their guests many memorable moments.

Natalia wore a full-skirted traditional wedding dress and carried a bouquet of calla lilies surrounded by large white feathers. She entered the ceremony to the strains of Tchaikovsky's *The Nutcracker*, which made her feel, she says, like a princess. Releasing doves from a wicker basket on the steps of London's Marylebone Register Office afterward was a special moment for the couple, symbolizing the moment of their union and the joining of their two families.

With several of their guests coming from abroad, the couple—whose family roots are in Russia and Hungary—wanted to show off the many highlights of the British capital as part of their celebrations. And a trip after the ceremony on the spectacular London Eye—the world's largest observation wheel—was certainly an original way to give everyone a taste of the city. They rented several of the Eye's glass pods for exclusive use, and enjoyed champagne and canapés as it made a leisurely circuit with London spread out before them in the sunshine.

Guests were transported the short distance from the ceremony to the River Thames and the London Eye in a red double-decker Routemaster bus, again giving everyone a great opportunity to see the sights. Using an unusual vehicle such as this to take guests from the ceremony to the reception venue is an inspired idea. It not only helps prevent the guests from getting lost en route, but also looks great in the wedding photographs.

The wedding reception was held at the super-stylish Hempel, one of London's original boutique hotels. The minimalist décor appealed to the couple, and they loved the white

ABOVE The couple's vintage Rolls Royce was adorned with white ribbon and a floral wreath of white summer flowers. **ABOVE CENTER** A single lily served as a name tag for each guest at the reception. **ABOVE RIGHT** Calla lilies were mixed with white feathers in the bride's bouquet. **OPPOSITE, LEFT** The bridesmaids wore pale blue beaded dresses and carried posies of pale pink roses. **OPPOSITE, RIGHT** The couple toasted each other on the London Eye, 450 feet above the city. **OPPOSITE, BELOW** Made of dark chocolate covered with white chocolate layers, the cake was displayed on a clear glass box filled with fresh pink rose petals.

color scheme and the light and airy rooms. The venue also has a beautiful garden that can be covered with a tent and is often used for celebrity parties. You may even recognize the setting from the film *Notting Hill*; it is where the lead characters, played by Julia Roberts and Hugh Grant, get married at the end of the film.

The *Swan Lake* theme came into its own at the reception, where two life-size ice swans were seen "swimming" on the pond in the hotel gardens, and the guests were given marzipan swans to greet them as they sat down for dinner. The couple made their entrance to the gardens through an archway of trailing pink orchids.

The reception tables were decorated with glass vases filled with slices of lime and topped with white roses or pink orchids and an abundance of feathers. Using slices of citrus fruit or lining the inside of glass containers with colored pebbles or leaves is a clever way to cover uninteresting flower stems and adds emphasis to the chosen color scheme.

Guests dined on an imaginative selection of Italian and Thai dishes prepared for them by the chef at I-Thai, the hotel's restaurant, with the addition of lots of Russian caviar, a particular favorite of both the bride and groom. A gypsy band entertained everyone throughout the meal with a repertoire of Hungarian and Russian love songs to reflect the couple's heritage.

MAIN PICTURE The gardens in front of The Hempel hotel were the setting for the pre-reception cocktail party, where guests enjoyed champagne and canapés. The *Swan Lake* theme was highlighted by two life-size ice swans decorated with floral wreaths that appeared to be "swimming" on the water. **ABOVE** Two white doves were released at the end of the marriage ceremony, symbolizing the union between the bride and groom and the joining of the two families.

country garden wedding *Cues from Nature*

Where is the ideal wedding location if the bride is
from Zimbabwe and the groom is from London?
For this couple the decision was easy: the sunshine
of South Africa proved irresistible.

Lindi Mabena and Robert Pitts created a day of sophisticated romance for family and
friends, who traveled from all over the world to watch them become husband and wife.

The fresh color theme of mint and zesty green set the tone for this stylish wedding;
a favorite color palette of the bride, it complemented the natural surroundings of the
vineyard venue. Green is an unusual choice for a wedding, but when coupled with plenty
of white and with the addition of brilliant sunshine, it is anything but drab.

If you have a favorite color, don't be afraid to choose it as the basis of your wedding
theme. Just about any color can be successful, provided that it is balanced by plenty of
white or ivory. But avoid using more than three colors in any scheme. You want your day
to look stylish, not theatrical.

Various different kinds of lilies, the bride's favorite flowers, also played a big part in
the decorations for the day, featuring in everything from Lindi's bouquet to the flower
arrangements at the ceremony and the centerpieces at the reception. The couple exchanged
their vows beneath a white gazebo surrounded by their guests, who were seated on chairs
covered in simple white covers. The gazebo was given an eye-catching topping, an eclectic
mixture of flower-filled glass vases and stone urns filled with white flowering plants. The
white fabric aisle runner leading up to the gazebo was strewn with fresh rose petals, and
the guests were given rose petals to use as confetti.

ABOVE Chinese lanterns encircled the tent; each one had a single flowerhead hanging from its center. **ABOVE RIGHT** The chocolate cake was a feast for the eyes; the bride took home the middle tier and the top tier was in fact fake, although it looked great! **ABOVE FAR RIGHT** Guests were greeted at the tables by a variety of colorful touches straight from nature such as this ornamental grass in a glass. **LEFT** The bride and groom were married in the venue gardens under a specially designed gazebo topped with vases of lilies and urns of white flowering plants.

The wedding took place at the 16th-century Allee Bleue wine estate in Franschhoek, a romantic setting surrounded by picturesque gardens with towering mountains in the distance. Once the ceremony was finished, guests enjoyed a late afternoon cocktail party on the lawns before joining Lindi and Robert for dinner in a canopy-covered courtyard.

Aleit, the couple's wedding planner, chose square rather than circular tables, which harmonized with the shape of the courtyard. The mint-green tablecloths were highlighted with a lime-green table runner and ivory linen napkins. The glass-cube centerpieces contained a variety of lilies, flesh-colored anthuriums, and miniature ivory roses with lime-green asclepias and foliage. Each vase was decorated with strips of thin ivory ribbon tied around the outside. All the wooden chairs had a padded ivory cushion.

The tent was cleverly spotlit using pink-toned lights that cast a soft, romantic glow over the area as the sun went down. Large Chinese lanterns also lit the edges of the tent, and the venue's famous 1,000-year old olive tree was bedecked in tiny fairy lights and served as the backdrop for the four-tiered wedding cake.

Instead of traditional favors, each of the wedding guests was given a luxury bag filled with a copy of the Sunday newspaper (hot off the press), a muffin, fruit, spring water and

ABOVE The tent in the courtyard was a spectacular setting for the reception. **OPPOSITE, ABOVE LEFT** Chairs were arranged in circles around the gazebo. **OPPOSITE, ABOVE RIGHT** A bunch of mini chrysanthemums, anthuriums, and local foliage awaited each guest at the tables. **OPPOSITE, BELOW LEFT** Lilies, anthuriums, and lime-green asclepias made up Lindi's bouquet. **OPPOSITE, BELOW RIGHT** The horse-drawn carriage was used to convey Lindi and Robert to the reception.

acetominephen for the anticipated hangovers! Guests were treated to a wonderful menu of international dishes, including line-fish malay topped with a walnut crust, gin and lime sorbet, sherry-marinated beef fillet with blue cheese and prune crust, and a dessert of ebony and ivory charlotte. They enjoyed selected wines from the venue's own cellars, as well as lots of water and grape juice topped with mint and strawberries to help beat the 108°F heat.

One of the best moments of the day for the bride was arriving in a horse-drawn carriage with her 83-year-old father. He had always maintained that he would never live to see his daughter married—so it was an extremely special moment for them both when he walked her down the petal-strewn aisle.

white wedding *English Castle*

This glorious white wedding took place on a perfect English summer's afternoon in the historical setting of Castle Ashby in Northamptonshire. It was truly a family affair—with the couple getting married, christening their baby daughter, and celebrating the bride's father's 70th birthday all on the same day.

A wedding with an all-white or all-cream color theme works beautifully when the venue needs minimal dressing or decoration and is as spectacular as Castle Ashby. It's a look that works well for a summer or winter wedding—dazzling in the sunshine, but equally stunning when lit by candles on a cold winter's day.

Karen Birch and Stephen Docherty chose the castle because they wanted somewhere that could be rented exclusively for the whole weekend; since it has its own church in the grounds, they could have the religious ceremony they both wanted without guests needing to travel between two separate venues. The main party arrived on Friday evening to celebrate the bride's father's birthday with a dinner held in the castle's dramatic Long Gallery.

There was no need for the services of a wedding planner since the couple had a strong sense of what they wanted from the outset. The bride, who admits to being fanatical about the details, sourced or made all of the many decorative touches, including the stationery, herself and, despite doing much of the venue dressing as well, describes it all as a "total pleasure."

The wedding took place on a hot summer afternoon in August. Once the wedding and christening ceremonies were over, guests spilled onto the castle's rolling lawns for champagne and canapés under a group of ancient oak trees. The area was transformed into an oasis of

ABOVE An amazing historic wedding venue, Castle Ashby dates back to 1574 and is still used as a family home by the Marquess of Northampton. **OPPOSITE, ABOVE LEFT AND RIGHT** In an unusual decorative touch, lanterns and flowers were tied with white ribbons and hung from the trees. **OPPOSITE, BELOW RIGHT** Violinists provided entertainment for guests at the garden cocktail reception. **OPPOSITE, BELOW LEFT** All the guests, even the youngsters, where given white disposable cameras with which to capture candid moments during the day.

cool tranquility, with white-clothed tables and white chairs, French daybeds, and voile drapes fluttering in the breeze. A multitude of white lanterns and flowerheads threaded onto white ribbons hung from the branches of the trees.

The florist made wonderfully fragrant centerpieces for the outdoor tables using a mass of white summer flowers bunched into pots and surrounded by sprigs of rosemary, then tied with bands of white ribbon. The castle's courtyard tables were decorated in the same way for the evening party. The reception was held in the castle's Great Hall, where there were just two very long, rectangular tables laid for dinner, again with an all-white theme. Rectangular tables have replaced round tables at many of the most fashionable weddings and look spectacular if the dimensions of the room allow for them to be laid end-to-end. Each chair was covered in white organdy, and the centerpieces were white rose heads sitting on mirrors and surrounded by candles interspersed with fragrant stocks and stephanotis. Each place setting was marked with a single sprig of lily of the valley or osteosperum with a sprig of rosemary. Once the meal was over, everyone enjoyed the perfect summer's evening in the castle courtyard, which was lit with white Chinese lanterns, fairy lights, and hundreds of flickering candles.

RIGHT AND OPPOSITE, ABOVE The castle courtyard made an atmospheric venue for the evening reception. In a tent with open sides, decked out with Chinese lanterns and fairy lights, guests danced the night away to a swing band. OPPOSITE, BELOW LEFT The rectangular dining tables featured centerpieces of mixed summer flowers. Each place setting was marked with a sprig of lily of the valley or osteosperum with rosemary. The chairs were covered in white organdy. OPPOSITE, BELOW RIGHT A talented friend made the wedding cake, an elaborate three-tiered extravaganza decorated and topped with fresh cream roses.

country wedding *Butterflies and Bagpipes*

A white clapboard house overlooking Cahas Mountain in Virginia, Sundara was the setting for the wedding of Kelly Pollard and Jason Paxton. The day was full of sunshine, laughter, and personal touches, such as the playing of the bagpipes, to reflect the bride's Irish ancestry, and a spectacular "butterfly release" by guests to mark memorable moments in the ceremony.

Guests received with their invitations a specially commissioned watercolor of Sundara, one of Virginia's premier wedding venues, which set the scene and doubled as a memento of the occasion. The marriage ceremony took place outdoors, in a naturally shady spot with views of the mountain. The reception was held in a large tent, subtly lit with colored spotlights, which flooded the whole area with various hues as the sun went down.

The color scheme was a chic summer palette of pinks, tangerines, and green, chosen by the bride and interpreted by the wedding coordinator, Posh Events. The scheme was reflected in every element of the day, from the fresh, striped tablecloths on the reception tables to the towers of limes stacked into tall, clear vases and used as the base for the centerpieces on the top table. The flowers were a glorious mixture of local species. Each of the guest tables had a slightly different arrangement of pink and orange flowers accented with zesty greens.

Guests were welcomed to the reception with signature cocktails, each a favorite tipple of the bride, the groom, or one of their parents. Each table was named after a destination visited by the couple during their relationship so far: the Caribbean table, the Beach table, the Bahamas table—and each featured a photo taken by the couple during their trip.

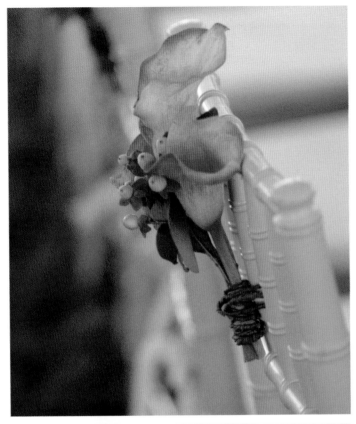

Dee Dixon and
Marvin Wills

St. Johns, Antigua

Harry and
Hask

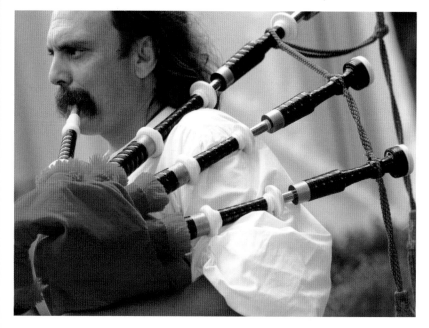

ABOVE The haunting sound of the bagpipes, played by a family friend, heralded the couple's arrival at the ceremony. **ABOVE LEFT** The ring bearer carried his precious cargo on a pillow covered by fresh flowers. **LEFT** The bridesmaids wore one-shouldered dresses in a shade of tangerine; the flowergirl's dress was tied with a matching tangerine sash, and she wore a circlet of fresh orange roses in her hair. **OPPOSITE, ABOVE LEFT** An orange calla lily was attached to the back of each chair. **OPPOSITE, BELOW LEFT** Butterflies were released at pertinent moments—for example, as the couple finished saying their vows. **OPPOSITE, ABOVE RIGHT** The bride's bouquet used spring and summer flowers grown locally in Virginia. **OPPOSITE, BELOW RIGHT** Placecards for guests, identifying their designated tables, were each decorated with a butterfly.

ABOVE A tent with open sides let in the sunshine and, later in the day, the evening air. **OPPOSITE, ABOVE** The spectacular, rectangular top table featured a series of tall and smaller floral arrangements, brimming with seasonal flowers. **OPPOSITE, BELOW RIGHT** As evening fell, the tent and nearby area was lit by colored spotlights, creating a magical quality in the trees. **OPPOSITE, BELOW LEFT** The tower of cupcakes on a wrought-iron stand added a "wow" factor as guests arrived at the party.

Placecards on the theme of butterflies helped guests to find their table. Rather than choose a traditional wedding cake, the couple opted for a contemporary tower of cupcakes; each cupcake was individually decorated with flowers to match the fresh flower decorations.

Once the formal part of the reception was over, guests were entertained by a live band playing a mixture of old favorites and requests from the floor. Throughout the evening guests were encouraged to write messages to Kelly and Jason in a handmade paper album. All of the guests had their pictures taken with a Polaroid camera, and the appropriate photograph was stuck in the album next to each message of good luck and congratulations.

This magical event culminated late in the evening with a spectacular firework display, plans for which had been kept a secret from everyone, including the groom, who has had a love of fireworks since he was a child.

big city wedding *Personal Touches*

A princess bride, heart-shaped wreaths, garlands of roses, a white Rolls–Royce, and candlelight: the union in Washington D.C. between Caroline Rochester and John Dickens is not far from perfection for anyone looking for the ultimate romantic wedding.

There is nothing quite like a black-tie dress code for creating a stylish event. Guests revel in the chance to dress up in glamorous outfits—and it was precisely such a mood of glamour that Caroline and John wanted to create for their celebrations at the famous St. Regis Hotel following their marriage at Holy Trinity Catholic Church in Georgetown.

Every detail was lovingly planned by the couple to combine family heritage and personal touches, and it culminated in a day brimming with originality and elegance. The color scheme was blush pink, and a monogram of the couple's intertwined initials was an integral theme, appearing on the stationery, the order of service, the napkins, the favors, and even the wedding cake. The overriding feeling the bride wanted to convey was one of "lush romance."

Personalizing your wedding using your initials is a relatively simple but highly effective way to stamp your style on the day. Monogrammed ribbon to tie up napkins, favors, and bouquets can be ordered through florists, and you can ask your cake-maker to incorporate your initials in the icing design. You could even ask your dress designer to work your initials into the trim on your dress or the decoration of your veil.

Flowers also played an important part in Caroline and John's wedding, principally a combination of gardenias and the bride's favorite blush- and champagne-colored roses. Romantic spring flowers such as hydrangeas, roses, peonies, sweet pea, and lilacs were used for texture and fragrance in the table arrangements. Heart-shaped wreaths made of roses were

romantic details

Everyone's idea of romance is different—it's more a feeling than a specific look to be copied. To create a romantic mood, use a palette of soft colors, delicate fabrics with flowing lines, and the timeless appeal of fragrant flowers. The soft glow of candlelight will instantly transform any venue, as will classical love songs and the muted clink of crystal champagne glasses.

ABOVE The bridal bouquet was a mixture of blush- and champagne-colored roses combined with gardenias in honor of the bride's late grandmother. **ABOVE RIGHT** Rose wreaths in the shape of hearts adorned the doors to the church. **ABOVE FAR RIGHT** Caroline wore an exquisitely beaded wedding gown accessorized with long white satin gloves, a diamond tiara, and a full-length veil. **OPPOSITE** The bride and groom traveled in luxurious style to the reception, enjoying the opulence of a vintage white Rolls–Royce.

placed on the doors of the church; buckets of roses lined the aisle; and the entrance was swagged with floral garlands. The bride's bouquet contained roses as well as several gardenias in honor of her late grandmother, who wore a gardenia corsage on her own wedding day.

Each of the petal-strewn reception tables was named after a Charles Dickens novel in acknowledgment of the fact that the groom is a descendant of the famous author. The top table, for example, was called *Great Expectations*. Every place setting had a blush-colored heart hanging from one of the glasses with the guest's name handwritten on it.

The wedding cake was a spectacular seven-tier extravaganza of coconut, chocolate, strawberries, lemon curd, and almond layers. Guests also enjoyed monogrammed cookies in the shape of the wedding cake with their coffee and champagne. Other memorable touches included a display table of photographs of the couple over the years, going back to when they were dating in high school, as well as photos from their parents' weddings. Each guest signed a piece of fabric, adding a good luck message to the bride and groom; the fabric has since been made into a quilt for the couple's new home. Guests were also given a personalized CD of some of Caroline and John's favorite music from the 1940s, including classics by Frank Sinatra and Dean Martin, to take home, along with a box of Krispy Kreme doughnuts!

LEFT The petal-covered tables were named after novels by Charles Dickens and decorated with towering, flower-decorated candelabra as well as smaller arrangements of hydrangeas, roses, peonies, lilac, and gardenias. **BELOW LEFT** The seven-tier cake was a mixture of coconut, strawberry, chocolate, almond, and lemon curd. **OPPOSITE, ABOVE LEFT** Buckets of pink and cream roses adorned the ends of the pews lining the aisle. **OPPOSITE, BELOW LEFT** The couple's monogram was used on everything from the order of service to the cake. **OPPOSITE, ABOVE RIGHT** Welcoming wreaths of fresh spring flowers were used to decorate the railings outside the church. **OPPOSITE, BELOW RIGHT** The bride and groom enchanted their guests with their first dance to Josh Groban's "You Raise Me Up."

For every couple seeking to create a day that's a little bit different, the contemporary wedding shows imagination and flair in every detail, from an unexpected theme to striking styling, and all the elements come together to create a maximum "wow" factor.

Contemporary

urban wedding *Black and White*

For the couple planning a contemporary wedding, there's nothing like using a black-and-white theme to give the day an instantly modern twist. It's a look that works at both formal and informal celebrations and is always popular with guests, who have an excuse to wear a glamorous tuxedo or a little black dress.

White has long been the most popular of wedding themes, but with the addition of black in all its drama, a wedding day takes on a completely different feel. And the effect of black is nowhere nearly as severe as might be imagined

The key to keeping the look feeling light, rather than funereal, is to make sure that white always remains the predominant color, with touches of black used as accents. Speak to all your key suppliers and note their suggestions for the stationery, the cake, the flowers, the table decorations, and even the menu. Creating a unique cocktail is always a fun idea. The coffee liqueur Kahlua is an obvious chice for a black and white wedding since it is very dark in color. A classic Black Russian—a heady concoction of vodka, Kahlua, milk, and Coca Cola—is guaranteed to get the party off to a lively start.

When choosing room and table decorations, it is advisable to use black in moderation. A black fabric table runner can enhance a crisp white linen tablecloth, or you could use black charger plates to set off classic white china. The flowers used in centerpieces should be white, but they can be displayed in black vases.

Aleit Swanepoel and Madri le Roux used a black-and-white theme to great effect at their wedding in Cape Town. They wanted to create a day that felt unique, individual, elegant, and relaxed, and to avoid stiff formality or giving the impression that they had tried too hard.

LEFT The bride—the only member of the bridal party to wear white—looked fabulous in her lace wedding dress with all-white bouquet. **ABOVE** Madri asked her florist to make trailing floral wrist corsages for her and her maids. **ABOVE CENTER** Male members of the bridal party each wore a white freesia as a boutonniere. **ABOVE RIGHT** All the stationery had a black-and-white theme, from the invitations to the individually designed order-of-service envelopes.

When you start planning a wedding, the first thing you need to do is to make a list, in order of importance, of all the things that will matter most on the day. Aleit and Madri's wish list read as follows: ambience, look and feel, setting, music, service, food, wine.

The warehouse-style venue they chose for the occasion had high ceilings, heavy wooden doors, wonderfully rich red walls, and Art Deco fixtures—all of which helped to create the French brasserie atmosphere they both wanted. The relaxed mood was a key feature of the whole day, from the character of the candlelit ceremony itself to the decision to have the speeches between the appetizer and main course rather than at the end of the meal.

The color theme was evident in the menu, with guests dining on scallop ravioli with squid ink butter, blackened beef with black truffle sauce, and Oreo tiramisu with dark toffee sauce. The wedding cake was decorated with black-and-white patterns. There were also six 12-inch high croquembouches, three filled with white chocolate and three with dark chocolate.

Entertainment was provided by a jazz band and a DJ. Wisely, Aleit and Madri made a list in advance of what they liked (Robbie Williams, George Michael, Kylie, Madonna) and what they didn't; musical tastes vary enormously, and the wrong style of music can ruin any reception. The couple wowed their guests with a first dance to Frank Sinatra's "Fly Me to the Moon."

LEFT Each of the six rectangular tables was laid with a black tablecloth, making a spectacular contrast with the rich red walls. Miniature black urns filled with white tulips alternated with tall candelabra along each table. BELOW LEFT The bride and groom wrote individual notes to all their guests; these doubled as place cards and were put into each guest's wine glass. OPPOSITE, ABOVE LEFT A five-tier design was chosen for the towering chocolate wedding cake. Each layer was decorated with a different black icing pattern. OPPOSITE, BELOW LEFT All the stationery had a delicate black lattice design on a white card, hand decorated with coordinating ribbon. At the church, each guest was given an envelope containing black and white confetti. OPPOSITE, ABOVE RIGHT Place settings were marked with decorated votives, each containing a candle. OPPOSITE, BELOW RIGHT The couple took to the checkered black-and-white dance floor to the strains of "Fly Me to the Moon" and "All of Me," both by Frank Sinatra.

black-and-white details

Black accents and details appeared in all elements of the wedding, including the dress code for the guests. Only the bride wore white. Aleit is one of South Africa's leading wedding planners, but left his own celebration in the capable hands of his team. "Sometimes you have to leave your work behind you, and I wanted to enjoy the experience of being a groom," he said.

LEFT The décor of the dining room used for the reception is an outstanding example of color theming at its best. Guests were seated at rectangular tables covered with white cloths and black lace overlays. The black cloths, chair covers, and black and white floor tiles contrast dramatically with the vibrant burnt-orange walls. The overhead lighting was turned off in favor of lighting from the tall silver candelabra and smaller votives that were a feature of each table—a clever device that instantly creates a romantic atmosphere. Centerpieces consisted of low bowls filled with white tulips that cascaded elegantly across the tables.

island wedding *Sunset Colors*

A palette of rich reds and oranges with accents of tropical green was the choice for this celebration in the Caymans. Famed for breathtaking scenery and sugar-white sands, the islands are also known for hurricanes, one of which nearly ruined the occasion.

The idea of the destination wedding—where a group of family and friends get together before the big day to celebrate the forthcoming nuptials—appealed to Cheri Carrington and Curt Hanson, doctors from Dallas, Texas. Their choice of venue was the Grand Old House on Grand Cayman, a former plantation house that is now a world-renowned restaurant. Thirty guests joined them for the week before the wedding and enjoyed scuba diving, shopping, and partying. Ninety more guests arrived for the rehearsal dinner the day before the wedding.

The wedding venue almost had to be changed a few months before the wedding after a devastating hurricane wreaked havoc on the island. But Cheri had fallen in love with it on a previous trip and was determined to go ahead. A huge amount of work by the islanders meant that the venue and the nearby beaches were transformed by the day of the wedding.

The marriage ceremony was performed by Cheri's grandfather, who had performed the same role for the bride's mother and two sisters. This became all the more meaningful in retrospect, when he passed away just four months after the wedding.

Cheri and her mother, Andrea, collaborated closely with the local wedding planner to make the most of the wonderful venue and incorporate as much local interest into the day as possible. The outdoor setting for both the ceremony and reception was a covered deck that stretched out over the ocean with views of the sunset. The ceiling and tent poles were draped in sheer white fabric with the addition of hundreds of twinkling fairy lights. Orange Chinese

RIGHT Every place setting had a Monstera leaf under a glass-beaded charger, and each guest's name was printed on a menu that doubled as a placecard. **BELOW RIGHT** Table centerpieces were glass vases of various heights and sizes filled with cymbidium orchids, pink and green roses, and gerberas. **OPPOSITE, ABOVE LEFT** All the stationery was custom-made in the wedding color scheme of burnt orange, red, and yellow. **OPPOSITE, BELOW LEFT** The bride was accompanied by two maids of honor (her sisters), five bridesmaids, and one flowergirl, all wearing dresses in shades of orange and carrying pomanders of green Yoko Ono chrysanthemums. **OPPOSITE, ABOVE RIGHT** All the male members of the bridal party wore cool linen shirts with a calla lily boutonniere. **OPPOSITE, BELOW RIGHT** The bride carried a bouquet of burnt-orange calla lilies and small orchids, some of which were threaded onto gold wire.

friends and breezes

Palm fans tied with silk ribbon were placed on all the guests' seats for the ceremony. Tied onto each fan was a card that read, "Good friends and a gentle breeze are blessings that make our hearts sing—Cheri & Curt."

ABOVE Guests dined by candlelight and illumination from the dozens of Chinese lanterns and hundreds of twinkling fairy lights. **OPPOSITE, ABOVE LEFT** A local harpist played throughout the ceremony. **OPPOSITE, BELOW LEFT** Each guest was given a detailed order of service, tied with a red ribbon. **OPPOSITE, ABOVE RIGHT** The bride's chocolate cake was decorated with fresh orchids and displayed on a zesty lime-colored tablecloth. **OPPOSITE, BELOW RIGHT** The groom had a cake of his own choice: key lime pie.

lanterns in different sizes were hung in varying lengths from the ceiling to sway in the breeze. The aisle runner for the ceremony consisted of white carpet covered with green petals.

Guests feasted on a menu of fresh local fare, including pan-seared crispy jumbo scallops on wild mushroom and leek ragout, and tenderloin of Angus beef or medallions of lobster flamed in brandy. For dessert there was a choice of two different cakes. The bride's cake was chocolate cake with chocolate icing (Cheri admits to being a chocoholic), and the groom's cake was key lime pie served with raspberry mango coulis.

Entertainment had a suitably tropical flavor, with a Caribbean band playing a mix of Caribbean, Cuban, and salsa music through the evening. The couple amazed everyone by leading the way with a salsa routine, having taken secret dancing lessons before the wedding. The evening finished with a fireworks display—something Cheri had wanted since childhood and a surprise gift from her parents. As her father gave a final toast, telling the couple always to keep "fire in their marriage," the pyrotechnics started—and so did the bride's tears!

zoo wedding *Animal Magic*

Germany's Hamburg Zoo was the unusual setting for the wedding of Claudia Luders and Gregor Gerlach. The groom's polo-playing friends, who arrived on their ponies, and a VIP guest in the form of a bejeweled elephant provided exotic touches.

This is a delightful example of a traditional wedding held in a thoroughly modern setting, representing the ideal approach for any couple planning a contemporary celebration. Claudia and Gregor wanted to enjoy a classic white wedding but include some elements that would surprise their guests—hence the decision to hold the ceremony and the reception in the grounds of Hamburg's famous zoo. It was the first time the zoo had been used for such an event, and it presented quite a logistical challenge since everything, from a fully equipped kitchen to the lavatories, had to be brought to the venue. But the couple had fallen in love with the place and felt it was well worth the effort.

Claudia, who had always loved the idea of a white wedding, made sure that everything in the reception tent was white, including tablecloths, chair covers, and linens. The table arrangements were white roses and lilies with just a hint of fresh green foliage. The chairs on the top table were each decorated with a garland of white roses. The tent was lit by hundreds of tall white candles and small votives to create a soft, romantic atmosphere.

The tent even had a white carpet, even though this meant that the builders had to wear plastic covers on their shoes for three days during preparations to keep it clean. The carpet was an indulgent touch, and the couple were resigned to the fact that it would probably be ruined by the end of the evening.

ABOVE The couple were delighted with their unusual guard of honor; they left the wedding ceremony under an arch formed by friends holding up polo sticks.
OPPOSITE, ABOVE LEFT A vintage Bentley adorned with a garland of fresh flowers transported the bride to the ceremony.
OPPOSITE, BELOW LEFT The bride's bouquet was a simple hand-held posy of cream roses. **OPPOSITE, ABOVE RIGHT** The flowergirl and pageboy were given baskets of fresh petals to use as confetti.
OPPOSITE, BELOW RIGHT The groom's polo-playing teammates surprised guests by arriving at the wedding on horseback.

The bride and groom left the ceremony under an archway of polo sticks, and several of the groom's polo-playing friends mingled with the guests on horseback. A magnificent elephant, complete with mahoot in formal attire, stood at the entrance to the zoo gardens, where the reception was held, to welcome the guests.

If the bride or groom is known to have a passion for a particular sport or an interesting hobby, it is an appealing personal touch to refer to it in the wedding celebrations. Ask your stationery company about incorporating relevant images of the sport or hobby in the invitations, menus, and placecards. References can also be included in the cake; there are cake-makers who are experts at making models in sugar as humorous cake-toppers.

After a champagne reception, Claudia and Gregor's guests dined on a four-course feast of ricotta and mushroom ravioli, turbot, roast venison, and curd-cheese dumplings with fresh berries and pistachio sorbet. A midnight snack of scrambled eggs with bacon and smoked salmon kept revelers happy as the party continued late into the night.

ABOVE A huge tent was erected in the zoo grounds. It had a wooden terrace so guests could enjoy views of the lake. **OPPOSITE, ABOVE LEFT** The all-white color scheme looked stunning in the white tent. **OPPOSITE, BELOW LEFT** The center of each table was decorated with fresh rose petals, foliage, and votives in glasses, all laid around an arrangement of roses and lilies. **OPPOSITE, ABOVE RIGHT** A garland of roses and hydrangeas adorned the couple's chairs. **OPPOSITE, BELOW RIGHT** A bejeweled elephant greeted guests at the reception.

magical moments

A "Wow!" factor venue is a must for many contemporary weddings. In this case, it reflected the couple's love of animals as well as providing a fabulous setting in the center of a city. Unusual elements, such as having an elephant to welcome the guests, kept everyone guessing what was coming next. The lakeside location for the tent, decked out in all-white livery, was the most glorious touch of all.

vineyard wedding *Under the Sun*

The Stellenbosch region of South Africa is home to some of the world's most beautiful vineyards and one of these, Plaisir de Merle, was the setting for the wedding of Mariken Claessens and Ruud Kooi. The day combined wonderful weather with a relaxed afternoon picnic and then a sumptuous dinner under a spectacular Bedouin-style tent.

The area where the ceremony was held was simply decorated with a white backdrop and oversized vases of white daisies and grasses. One distinctive touch was the "faces" artwork that adorned the setting. The image of two faces with Table Mountain in the background and the sea at the front was conceived by the bride and groom and created by a design professional. The image will now be used as a logo for all special occasions in their lives, including birth announcements, anniversaries, and important family gatherings.

The wedding guests sat on white chairs in the sunshine as the couple exchanged vows framed by trees and the mountains in the background. The late morning ceremony was followed by a picnic on the lawns behind the wine cellars, with the guests sitting on cushions on the grass, shaded by white parasols, being entertained by a jazz quartet who strolled among the tables responding to requests.

The picnic was packed into individual boxes decorated with lime-green tissue paper and lime ribbon. Guests sipped sparkling wine from individual mini-bottles topped with colorful straws. Younger guests had their own special picnic boxes that, apart from food, included a butterfly net, a bottle of bubbles, and a Frisbee. After an afternoon of fun and games and swimming, Mariken and Ruud invited their adult guests to a sit-down dinner.

Love and Laughter The couple exchanged their marriage vows in a simple ceremony in perfect spring sunshine. They both wanted to create a relaxed day full of love and laughter with unforgettable touches that their guests would remember forever. There were to be no standard wedding themes, no rigid schedules, and no formality. Guests started the evening with a selection of "sundowner" cocktails. To encourage an informal atmosphere, guests were served their appetizer and dessert by wait staff, but were asked to go up to the *braii* (spit-roast) for their main course. The chardonnay and merlot wines that accompanied the dinner both came from the Plaisir de Merle vineyard.

ABOVE During the marriage ceremony, in keeping with the relaxed theme, Mariken and Ruud were surrounded by simple glass vases filled with white daisies and ornamental grasses. **ABOVE RIGHT** The specially commissioned "faces" artwork has since been adopted as the family logo. **LEFT** The bride and groom departed from the ceremony amid a shower of confetti and good wishes.

The tent had a white base and was set with two rectangular tables and modern white chairs. The tables were decorated with trays of miniature candles and glass vases filled with gerberas and lilies resting on whitewashed trays. Everything else was kept white and simple. Fairy lights were strung along the frame of the tent to give soft, romantic lighting as night fell. Several small decorative lily ponds were dotted around the canopy. Once dinner was finished, the tented area was the perfect place for guests to relax. The newlyweds took to a specially laid dance floor in the garden, where they kicked off the more energetic part of the evening with their first dance to "My Baby Just Cares for Me" by Nina Simone.

Buffet-style eating is a feature of many contemporary wedding receptions and, as long as there are plenty of tables and chairs so that guests don't have to use one hand to feed themselves while balancing their plates in the other, the buffet meal is ideal for a relaxed occasion. If your wedding party includes a number of older guests, it's a good idea to have wait staff on hand to carry plates back to the seating area if anyone is having difficulties. To prevent lines, have at least two serving stations and encourage guests to use them both.

RIGHT The couple exchanged vows in the sunshine, with friends and family seated on the grass around them. OPPOSITE, ABOVE The cake was made of decadent Belgian chocolate decorated with swirls of white chocolate and lime-green flowerheads. OPPOSITE, BELOW LEFT Guests sat on floor pillows and benches to enjoy their picnic lunch in comfort. Vases filled with ornamental grasses were dotted about on the lawn. OPPOSITE, BELOW RIGHT Strolling jazz musicians offered entertainment throughout the afternoon.

LEFT The evening reception was held under an ultra-modern canopy with open sides. Some 70 guests dined at two long tables covered in white tablecloths, with matching contemporary chairs in classic white. The happy couple made their entrance to the sound of "Beautiful Day" by U2. **BELOW** Each table was decorated with pebble-filled trays of tiny candles alternated with glass containers on whitewashed trays containing white lilies and gerberas.

boutique wedding *Minimalist Chic*

Small is beautiful was the theme for the chic London wedding of Jennifer Freedman and Anthony Mielnik. The couple were intent on creating an intimate day for their immediate family in the city's favorite boutique hotel, with style details and personal touches sourced from their travels around the world.

Getting married is a very personal occasion, and not every couple wants a big wedding. It may be that you would prefer to celebrate in front of just your close family and friends. When planning a small wedding, attention to detail can be even more important than at a large one because there are fewer elements for your guests to focus on. A 'less is more' approach will probably be the most successful, but every detail matters; you want your friends to think they are coming to a select party—and the good news is that your budget will go farther since you have fewer people to entertain.

The Hempel Hotel, the couple's choice of venue, is renowned as a temple to minimalist chic. The cream décor is very simple; the only decoration is provided by pots of Phaelanopsis orchids, and the only other color in the venue is black. Jennifer, who is American, and Anthony, who is from Australia, wanted to create a non-traditional day that felt comfortable and reflected their true personalities. The dress code was definitely relaxed; the groom's nephew wore shorts and flip-flops!

Jennifer and Anthony were eager to be totally involved with every detail and happily made their own invitations, thank-you cards, menus, and placecards. They wrote the vows for their civil ceremony under the Eiffel Tower, then traveled all over Paris to find the perfect cigars for their guests to enjoy before jetting off to Barcelona, Malta, and Miami to find their outfits.

ABOVE The bride wore a lace-encrusted strapless dress from Creazioni Elena in Malta, and the groom found his Marc Jacobs jacket, Dolce & Gabbana satin shirt, and Gucci trousers in Barcelona. OPPOSITE, ABOVE The room for the ceremony was an oasis of tranquility, with linen-covered chairs and the soft glow of candlelight. OPPOSITE, BELOW LEFT Each place setting at the reception reflected the Asian fusion menu and had traditional flatware as well as bamboo chopsticks. OPPOSITE, BELOW RIGHT The Belgian chocolate wedding cake was covered with white chocolate and decorated with white chocolate fans.

The straightforward but very personal ceremony was conducted in the hotel, with guests seated on chairs covered in white linen and surrounded by a selection of glowing candles. The entire wedding party then moved on to I-Thai, the Hempel's famous restaurant, to enjoy one of the establishment's Asian Fusion menus. The black wooden tables were decorated in Asian style with white china, bamboo chopsticks, and long black oak boxes filled with wax beads and candles as centrepieces. Beside each plate was a matt silver picture holder containing the placecard. The hotel's florist decorated the dining area with white orchids and dozens of scented white candles and votives.

The menu started with honey-spiced duck and pan-roasted scallops with peanut pesto, followed by tomato risotto, fillet of beef in red wine, and poached lobster with lotus noodles and snake beans. Dessert was the decadent Belgian chocolate truffle wedding cake, covered in white chocolate with white chocolate fans on top.

Everyone enjoyed a leisurely meal with plenty of champagne before waving the newlyweds off on their Barbados honeymoon.

Modern Classic The most
important thing to remember when planning your
wedding is that it's your day and it should be designed
to reflect your own hopes and dreams rather than to
please everyone else. Jennifer and Anthony wanted
an intimate family occasion, and those closest to them
were happy to go along with this. The wedding was a
reflection of their love of contemporary fashion coupled
with relaxed informality. It was an occasion devoid of
many of the traditional trappings, but it was a wonderful
affirmation of their personal style—and they happily
admit that they wouldn't have changed a thing.

nature wedding *Circle of Love*

For a couple with a very laid-back approach to life, the Matara Centre, a spiritual retreat hidden in the depths of rural England, was the perfect choice for their wedding celebrations.

On their first visit to the Matara Centre, Helen Vickers and Kevin O'Rourke knew they had found their dream venue because it combined their love of simplicity with a truly spectacular setting amid 27 acres of Cotswolds countryside.

This is the perfect example of a wedding venue that needs minimal decoration and actively benefits from a "less is more" approach. The buildings and the gardens all have a strong identity, and couples choosing such a venue should work subtly to enhance what is already there rather than introducing a strong theme of their own. The same rules apply to period locations with distinctive architecture: use history as your theme and work with the venue's color palette to achieve style and harmony.

The organization of the wedding was something of a busman's holiday for the bride since she had recently set up her own wedding planning business, but it was the ideal opportunity to indulge her creativity to achieve her own perfect day.

Helen didn't want the wedding to have a set theme, but decided to use her favorite flower, the Phalaenopsis orchid, as the principal style influence. Images of the orchid appear on the stationery (which the couple designed and made themselves), and the flowers themselves are included in the bride's bouquet, in the boutonnieres and corsages, on the reception tables and as a decoration on the wedding cake. Helen's chosen color scheme was a mixture of ivory, French navy, and fuchsia pink.

Natural Light One of the more spectacular touches that impressed the guests was the domed ceiling of the reception room. The bride made the most of this amazing space by hanging orchid flowers and crystals on long strands of silver wire so they sparkled in the sunlight.

The marriage ceremony reflected Helen and Kevin's love of music from around the world. The bride made her entrance to the South American song "The Girl from Ipanema." The couple signed the register to a Hawaiian version of "Somewhere over the Rainbow" and walked back down the aisle to Marvin Gaye's "How Sweet It Is to Be Loved by You." Later, at the reception, their first dance song was an Irish fiddle solo, Van Morrison's "Sweetest Thing."

One of the most memorable elements of the ceremony was a reading from *Ulysses* by James Joyce; this was an edited version of the final paragraphs of the book, where one of the characters is describing how her husband proposed to her. The originality of the reading made for a tear-jerking few minutes for everyone there.

The couple were eager to keep the atmosphere informal during the sumptuous wedding feast, so the guests served themselves from a black lacquered Lazy Susan placed in the center of each table. Wines included Bollinger champagne, New Zealand sauvignon blanc, and South African cabernet merlot, all sourced during a pre-wedding visit to France. Each of the adults was welcomed to the table with a miniature bottle of Tequila (complete with worm) as a thank-you for attending; children were given organic chocolate piranhas.

Entertainment was provided throughout the day by a versatile swing band that played Irish tunes during the cocktail reception and meal, and then a wide range of dance music in the evening; the dance floor was packed all night. Pinatas filled with chocolates were hung in trees around the venue to keep the smaller guests entertained. As night fell, the party moved to the large house next door to the venue, which the couple had rented and where many of the guests were staying, where revels continued until dawn.

ABOVE AND PREVIOUS PAGE The Matara Centre is a spiritual retreat. In its grounds are many structures with an Eastern influence, which provide fantastic backdrops for photographs. RIGHT Colorful tribal masks hang from the branches of trees close to the center. OPPOSITE, ABOVE RIGHT All the stationery, from the invitations to the order of service, were made by the couple and decorated with an orchid motif. OPPOSITE, BELOW RIGHT The bride's dress was made by designer Jenny Packham, and she carried a simple stem of white orchids adorned with crystals. Her maid of honor wore a softly draped dress from Ritzou. OPPOSITE, ABOVE LEFT AND BELOW LEFT Orchid designs and orchid sprigs were used to decorate the four-tier wedding cake by Eric Lanard, an award-winning patisserie specialist.

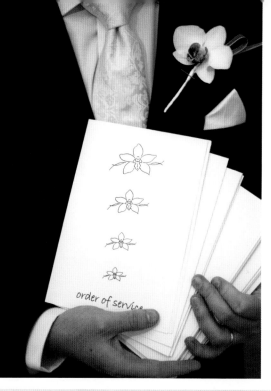

sunshine wedding *Summer Simplicity*

The modern wedding is very much about creating a celebration that reflects your personalities—and not all couples want a day filled with tradition and formality. Shai Chen and Willem le Roux are one pair who went for something different; they planned a day that oozed contemporary style as well as refreshing simplicity.

Simple definitely doesn't have to mean ordinary when it comes to planning a contemporary wedding. In many ways, if you adopt a "less is more" approach, the style details become even more important than at a conventional wedding because, even though there are fewer of them, they are the focus of everyone's attention. Shai and Willem were determined that their wedding should look stunning but have a relaxed atmosphere with few speeches and no formalities.

The couple, both from Cape Town, wanted a religious ceremony and were lucky enough to find a church in a minimalist setting with simple whitewashed walls and benches and a wooden floor that perfectly suited their relaxed theme. They didn't want traditional flower arrangements, so their florist did a wonderful job decorating the church using large, plain glass vases filled with upside-down arum lilies. She also decorated the windowsills with white candles and attached white orchids to a white screen around the altar. At the entrance to the church, guests could help themselves to containers of confetti made from white rose petals and fresh mint.

After the ceremony, the wedding party moved to the Vrede en Lust wine estate for an informal cocktail reception and cake-cutting ceremony in the summer sunshine. Dispensing with tradition and having the speeches and cake-cutting before the main meal is a growing trend at informal weddings. If no one has to worry about having to make a speech after the meal, it means that all the guests can enjoy the evening in relaxed fashion.

ABOVE In the pared-down church interior, the bride and groom were flanked by white plinths displaying vases of upside-down arum lilies. ABOVE RIGHT Guests sat on simple white benches, each one decorated with a single flowerhead. OPPOSITE, LEFT At a pre-reception cocktail party, informal hand-tied bunches of roses and orchids were suspended from the branches of trees. OPPOSITE, RIGHT The bride's bouquet consisted of white tulips wrapped in aspidistra leaves; the bridemaid's posy contained pink proteas.

The reception was held in the vineyard's 220-year-old Historic Cellar, where Aleit, the couple's wedding planner, suggested using a single long table to seat all 100 guests—creating a definite "wow" factor as everyone arrived at the venue. The table setting was simple: a crisp white linen tablecloth lined with alternating candles and cube vases filled with tulips, orchids, or proteas. The contemporary white chairs each had a brilliant-red seat cushion, and the room was cleverly lit by a mixture of spotlights and candles.

The bride and groom arrived to greet their guests to the strains of "Come Fly with Me" by Michael Buble. Proceedings got under way with an introduction by the two best men and, in keeping with the informal approach, short speeches were delivered between courses.

To conclude the party, everyone was invited out into the garden, where a tent, complete with checkered dance floor and a comfortable seating area, had been erected as the venue for the rest of the evening. At midnight, everyone enjoyed a feast of chocolate brownies, vanilla fudge, pistachio macaroons, and hazelnut and almond nougat.

RIGHT A spectacular tent was erected in the grounds, in which people could dance and relax after the reception. It was fully fitted out with a checkered dance floor, ottomans and sofas, and lit with oversize Chinese lanterns. OPPOSITE, ABOVE A single table seated all 100 guests. OPPOSITE, BELOW LEFT The carrot and nut cake was served as dessert with either white chocolate sabayon or white chocolate custard. OPPOSITE, BELOW RIGHT Each place setting was decorated by a candle, an orchid, or a cube vase containing yellow tulips or proteas.

Wedding Details

Each of the couples whose wedding is featured in the book worked closely with a group of carefully selected wedding suppliers. Details of the main contributors are listed on the following pages to inspire you as you plan your own beautiful wedding.

Traditional

MICHELE AND JEFFREY *pages 16–23*
photographers Roy Llera and Amber Temkin (www.royllera.com)
wedding planner Dascal Karla (www.karlaevents.com)
venue Villa Vizcaya (www.vizcaya.com)
catering and flowers Karla Conceptual Events (www.karlaevents.com)
wedding cake Ana Paz (www.cakesbyanapaz.com)
wedding dress Vera Wang (www.verawang.com)
favors Michele Watches (www.michele.com)

SONITA AND JONATHAN *pages 24–29*
photographer Lovegrove Photography (www.lovegrovewedding.com)
wedding planner Time4You (www.time4you.co.uk)
venue Highclere Castle (www.highclerecastle.co.uk)
florist Passion Flowers (www.flowersbypassion.co.uk)
catering Andy Varma (www.vama-direct.co.uk)
wedding cake Choccywoccydoodah (www.choccywoccydoodah.com)
bride's and bridesmaids' dresses Toni-Anne (www.toni-anne.co.uk)
stationery Magnakarta (www.magnakarta.com)

KATIE AND BRAD *pages 30–37*
photography Julie Mikos (www.juliemikos.com)
wedding planner Grace Dougan (www.atouchofgrace.biz)
venue The Old Federal Reserve (www.noehill.com/sf/landmarks/sf158.asp)
florist Katherine Oliver at Cherries (www.cherriesflowers.com)
catering Union Street Catering (www.unionstreetcatering.com)
wedding cake Jill Branch (www.branchingoutcakes.com)
wedding dress Jane Hamidi at Palazzo (www.palazzo.com)
veil Amy Michelson (www.amymichelson.com)
flowergirls' dresses Laura Ashley (www.lauraashley-usa.com)
stationery Paper Source (www.paper-source.com)
calligraphy Tracy Joe (www.tracyjoe.com)

STEPHANIE AND RAPHAEL *pages 38–45*
photographer Julie Mikos (www.juliemikos.com)
venue Beaulieu Gardens (www.bvwines.com)
florist Julie Stevens at Julies Flowers (www.juliestevensdesign.com)
catering Elaine Bell Catering (www.elainebellcatering.com)
wedding cake Perfect Endings (www.perfectendings.com)
wedding dress Atelier des Modistes (www.atelierdesmodistes.com)
groom's tuxedo Tommy Hilfiger (www.tommyhilfiger.com)

KRISTIN AND DANIEL *pages 46–51*
photographer Julie Mikos (www.juliemikos.com)
wedding planner Laura Schoolcraft (www.patrickdavids.com)
venue James Leary Flood Mansion (www.floodmansion.com)
florist Eunice Venetta (www.pairsandpieces.com)
catering Patrick David Fine Catering (www.patrickdavids.com)
wedding cake Julie Durkee, Torino Baking (www.torinobaking.com)
wedding dress Marisa (www.marisabridals.com)
bridesmaids' dresses Kathlin Argiro (www.kathlinargiro.com)
stationery Hyegraph Invitations (www.hyegraph.com)

SUSANNE AND DARREN *pages 52–59)*

photographer Contre-Jour (www.contre-jour.co.uk)
wedding planner Kathryn Lloyd Wedding Design (www.kathrynlloyd.co.uk)
venue Villa Belrose, St Tropez (www.villabelrose.com)
florist Monceau Fleurs (www.monceaufleurs.com)
wedding cake Hotel Sacher (www.sacher.com)
stationery Chartula Stationery (www.chartula.co.uk)
wedding dress Catherine Walker (www.catherinewalker.com)

REIKO AND RICHARD *pages 60–67*

photographer Joanne Dunn Photographers (www.joannedunn.it)
wedding planner Barbara Bertini-Platt, Weddings International
(www.italianwedding.com)
venue Hotel Caruso (www.hotelcaruso.com)
florist Armando Malafronte (www.malafronte.com)
catering Hotel Caruso (www.hotelcaruso.com)
wedding dress Monique Lhuillier (www.moniquelhuillier.com)
stationery I Do Invitations (www.Idoinvitations.com)

Romantic

ALEX AND TIM *pages 68–75*

photography English Rose (www.englishroseweddings.co.uk)
wedding planner Songbird Events (www.songbirdevents.com)
flowers Covent Garden Flower Market (www.cgma.gov.uk/flowers.htm)
wedding dress Wizard of Gos (www.thewizardofgos.co.uk)
bridesmaids' dresses The Cross (020 7727 6760)
flowergirls' dresses Monsoon Accessorize (www.monsoon.co.uk)
birdcages/butterflies/garlands Lavenders of London
(www.lavendersoflondon.com)

NATALIA AND VIOREL *pages 76–81*

photographer Lovegrove Photography (www.lovegrovewedding.com)
venue The Hempel (www.the-hempel.co.uk)
florist Paula Pryke (www.paula-pryke-flowers.com)
wedding cake Café Amato (www.amato.co.uk)
wedding dress Endrius at Harrods (www.endrius.com)
bridesmaids' dresses Maria Grachvogel at Debenhams (www.debenhams.com)
routemaster bus Timebus Travel (www.timebus.co.uk)
entertainment The London Eye (www.londoneye.com)

LINDI AND ROB *pages 82–87*

photographer Joe Dreyer (www.joe.co.za)
wedding planner Aleit Wedding Co-Ordination (www.aleit.co.za)
venue Allee Bleue Wine Estate (www.alleebleue.com)
florist Okasie (www.okasie.co.za)
catering Platter Perect (www.corneronqueens.co.za)
wedding dress Prima Donna Brides (www.primadonnabridal.co.uk)
stationery The Wedding Works (www.theweddingworks.co.za)
horse and carriage Wine Valley Horse Trails (www.horsetrails-sa.co.za)

KAREN AND STEVE *pages 88–93*

photographer Rachel Barnes (www.rachelbarnes.co.uk)
venue Castle Ashby (www.castleashby.co.uk)
florist Lisa Daly at Castle Ashby
wedding dress Stephanie Allin (www.oneandonly.co.uk)
bridesmaids' dresses Berketex Bride (www.bb.com)
entertainment Gary Williams (www.garywilliams.co.uk)

KELLY AND JASON *pages 94–99*

photography Rodney Bailey (www.rodneybailey.com)

wedding planner Caroline Hammond, Posh Events
(www.posheventplanners.com)

venue Sundara (www.mysundara.com)

catering Centre Stage Food (www.centrestagefood.com)

wedding cake Centre Stage Food (www.centrestagefood.com)

CAROLINE AND JOHN *pages 100–105*

photographer Rodney Bailey (www.rodneybailey.com)

wedding planners Amy Barone, Northern VA Bridal Services
(www.novabridal.com)

venue St Regis Hotel, Washington (www.starwoodhotels.com)

florist Nick Perez (www.nicksflowers.com)

wedding cake Fancy Cakes by Leslie (www.fancycakesbyleslie.com)

bridal cookies Bundles of Cookies (www.bundlesofcookies.com)

wedding dress Reem Acra (www.reemacra.com)

bridesmaids' dresses Lazaro (www.lazaro.com)

stationery Crane Paper (www.crane.com)

Contemporarry

MADRI AND ALEIT *pages 108–15*

photography Jean-Pierre Uys (www.jeanpierrephotography.co.za)

wedding planner Aleit Wedding Co-ordination (www.aleit.co.za)

venue Ginja and Shoga, Cape Town (www.dining-out.co.za)

florists Flowers in the Foyer (www.flowersinthefoyer.co.za), Okasie
(www.okasie.co.za), Paradiso (www.paradiso.co.za)

wedding cake Cakes by Wade (www.wadescakes.co.za)

stationery Elsje Designs (www.elsjedesigns.co.za)

CHERI AND CURT *pages 116–21*

photography David Wolfe Photography (www.davidwolfephotography.com)

venue The Grand Old House (www.grandoldhouse.com)

wedding planner Celebrations (www.celebrationsltd.com)

wedding cake and flowers Celebrations (www.celebrations.com)

wedding dress Ristarose (www.ristarose.com)

groom's outfit Hickey Freeman (www.hickeyfreeman.com)

CLAUDIA AND GREGOR *pages 122–27*

photography Ian Johnson (www.ianjohnsonphoto.co.uk)

venue Hamburg Zoo (www.hagenbeck.de)

florist Blumen Graaf (www.blumengraaf.de)

catering Landhaus Scherrer (www.landhausscherrer.de)

wedding cake Sweet Dreams (www.sweet-dreams-confiserie.de)

wedding dress Vera Wang (www.verawang.com)

favors Martha Stewart (www.marthastewart.com)

MARIKEN AND RUUD *pages 128–35*

photography Jean-Pierre Uys (www.jeanpierrephotography.co.za)

wedding planner Aleit Wedding Co-ordination (www.aleit.co.za)

venue Plaisir de Merle (www.plaisirdemerle.co.za)

florist Okasie (www.okasie.co.za)

catering Extreem Kwizeen (www.extreemzwizeen.co.za)

picnic catering The Picnic Company (www.picnics.co.za)

wedding cake Kanya Hunt (www.celebrationhouse.co.za)

stationery The Wedding Works (www.theweddingworks.co.za)

tent Ukuba Afrika (www.ukubaafrika.co.za)

JENNIFER AND ANTHONY *pages 136–41*
photography Lovegrove Photography (www.lovegroveweddings.com)
venue The Hempel (www.the-hempel.co.uk)
catering I-Thai (www.the-hempel.co.uk)
wedding cake Choccywoccydoodah (www.choccywoccydoodah.com)
wedding dress Creazioni Elena (www.creazionielana.it)
groom's outfit Jacket/Marc Jacobs (www.marcjacobs.com) Shirt/Dolce & Gabbana (www.dolceandgabbana.com) and shirt/Gucci (www.gucci.com)

HELEN AND KEVIN *pages 142–47*
photographer Lovegrove Photography (www.lovegroveweddings.com)
wedding planner Eat, Drink, Get Married (www.eatdrinkgetmarried.com)
venue The Matara Centre (www.matara.co.uk)
florist Frances Fenwick (www.francesfenwick.co.uk)
catering Relish Catering, Cirencester (01285 658444)
wedding cake Eric Lanard at Savoir Design (www.savoirdesign.co.uk)
wedding dress Jenny Packham (www.jennypackham.com)
entertainment Dizzy Club (www.dizzy-club.co.uk)

SHAI AND WILLEM *pages 148–53*
photographer Jean-Pierre Uys (www.jeanpierrephotography.co.za)
wedding planner Aleit Wedding Co-Ordination (www.aleit.co.za)
venue Vrede en Lust Wine Centre (www.vnl.co.za)
florist Floral Design Studio (www.flowerfloraldesign.co.za)
caterers Salt and Pepper Catering (www.saltandpeppercatering.co.za)
wedding cake Kanya Hunt (www.celebrationhouse.co.za)
tent Chattels (www.chattels.co.za)

Index

Acknowledgments and Credits

Carole Hamilton would like to thank all the couples who have shared their beautiful weddings in this book. She would also like to thank all the photographers, listed below, for providing their fabulous images.

CONTRE-JOUR PHOTOGRAPHY
www.contre-jour.co.uk
18 New Quebec Street
London W1H 7RX, UK
Pages 52–59.

DAVID WOLFE PHOTOGRAPHY
www.davidwolfephotography.com
Pages 116–21.

IAN JOHNSON
www.ianjohnsonphoto.com
+ 44 (0)1206 543 589
London Los Angeles Stockholm
Pages 5 right, 11 above left, 122–27.

JEAN-PIERRE UYS PHOTOGRAPHY
Cape Town
South Africa
www.jeanpierrephotography.co.za
+ 27 84 5774686
Pages 5 center, 7 center left, 7 below
left, 11 above right, 108–115, 128–35, 148–53.

JOANNE DUNN
www.joannedunn.it
Pages 60–67.

'JOE' PHOTOGRAPHER
www.joe.co.za
joe@joe.co.za
+ 27 82 5499885
Pages 7 above center, 7 above right,
7 below center, 11 below, 82–87.

JOHN & JILL ENGLISH
English Rose Weddings
www.englishroseweddings.co.uk
+ 44 (0)1531 660559
Pages 4–5 below left, 7 center,
68–75, 157 center.

JULIE MIKOS PHOTOGRAPHY
www.juliemikos.com
Pages 2, 5 above left, 8, 14–15,
30–37, 38–45, 46–51.

LOVEGROVE PHOTOGRAPHY
www.lovegroveweddings.com
Pages 5 below center, 7 above left, 7 below
right, 24–29, 76–81, 106–107, 136–41,
142–47, 157 below.

RACHEL BARNES PHOTOGRAPHY
www.rachelbarnes.co.uk
enquiries@rachelbarnes.co.uk
+ 44 (0)1832 720154
Pages 88–93.

RODNEY BAILEY
Wedding photojournalism
www.rodneybailey.com
Pages 4, 13, 66–67, 94–99, 100–105,
157 above.

ROY LLERA PHOTOGRAPHY
www.royllera.com
11510 NE 2nd Avenue
Miami, FL 33161
USA
+ 1 305 759 2600
Pages 7 center right, 18–23.